HUMAN
KINDNESS

HUMAN
KINDNESS

Edited by Renée Hollis

TIMELESS WISDOM
True stories that reveal the depths of the human experience

Emotional Inheritance

First published 2019

Emotional Inheritance
An imprint of Exisle Publishing Pty Ltd
PO Box 864, Chatswood, NSW 2057, Australia
226 High Street, Dunedin, 9016, New Zealand
www.exislepublishing.com

A CiP record for this book is available from the National Library of Australia.

ISBN 978-1-925820-05-8

Designed by Nada Backovic
Typeset in 12/18 Sabon Lt Std
Printed in China

This book uses paper sourced under ISO 14001 guidelines from well-managed forests and other controlled sources.

10 9 8 7 6 5 4 3 2 1

How far that little
candle throws his
beams! So shines
a good deed in a
weary world.

WILLIAM SHAKESPEARE

CONTENTS

Wise sayings often
fall on barren ground,
but a **kind** word is
never thrown away.

ARTHUR HELPS

INTRODUCTION

Every day in the news we hear remarkable true stories that demonstrate the resilience of the human spirit. We thought it was time that more of these stories were heard, so we organized an international short story writing competition, which has resulted in the publication of the Timeless Wisdom collection of books.

We were overwhelmed by the variety and richness of the hundreds of entries from around the world. Our criteria for final selection were that the stories should reflect a diversity of writing, blend humour and pathos, and balance moments of drama with those of quiet contemplation.

Kindness comes in many forms and affects all of us. As Mark Twain said, 'Kindness is the language which the deaf can hear and the blind can see.' And while a kind gesture can often simply make someone feel better about their day, sometimes — as the stories collected here show — it can save lives. From the woman who stopped a suicidal man from jumping just by taking the time to listen to him, to the couple who fostered a baby they found abandoned in a rubbish bin when no one else could help; from the students who came to the rescue of an elderly man fallen on black ice, to the response of a terrorist leader when confronted by a young child's cries for her favourite doll — these are stories of unexpected kindness that have had a lasting impact on the storyteller.

Interspersed between these stories are quotes about kindness by people as diverse as William Shakespeare, Mark Twain, Jesse Jackson, Mother Teresa and J.M. Barrie. The result is a book that explores all that is best about human nature.

WOLF

Sue Corke

He had caught my attention. I looked again at the bedraggled figure in front of me, his face taut and greenish in the bad subway light, eyes unfocused, his slight body slumped against the wall. Just as I put my token in the slot, he called out to no one in particular that he was going to jump, that this was the end. He pulled himself up and stumbled down the steps towards the platform. I was in no doubt about his intentions. I yelled at the ticket guy, trapped behind his glass, to get help.

I flung myself through the turnstile, overtaking him as he reached the bottom of the stairs, the sound of my high heels hollow on the cement.

'Hold on,' I squeaked, scared and shaky. 'What's going on? Help is coming.' I manoeuvred my bulky briefcase to block the path. I took a hard look at him. He was sobbing now, a small, bony man in a mud-streaked grey jacket and dirty jeans, ripped around his ankles. He must have been about 50 although he was shopworn and it was hard to be precise. I took out a Kleenex and gave it to him.

'What's wrong? What's your name?' I asked, introducing myself.

'Just leave me alone,' he snuffled. 'Go away. It hurts so bad. It's the lupus. I've made up my mind. You can't stop me.'

'We can get you to a hospital. It'll be okay,' I ventured. It sounded weak and inadequate. I was out of my depth, painfully so.

The train came screeching through the tunnel and down the track, into the station. My single focus was to prevent him from getting past me, from doing what he wanted to do. He made no move but I couldn't let my guard down. I kept up a meaningless chatter. Each time a train came in I stiffened and prepared for a physical encounter.

His name was John Elias Wolf. He had been ill for months, he said. He couldn't work any more; his kids hated him and his wife had left him; he couldn't pay his rent and had just been evicted. His meds weren't working. He just wanted it all to end.

I wouldn't normally have been at that subway station so early on a February evening. I had a moment of self-pity. I wasn't having such a great day either. I had just been fired by my latest shrink. She said I was wasting her time, finding anything and everything to talk about except what was really going on with my ex and my rampant daughter. I had slammed out of her office after 10 minutes, vaguely wondering if she would charge me for the whole hour, scrabbling in my purse for a subway token, angry and disappointed both at myself and at her. I pondered how surreal it was to switch roles from patient to counsellor in the precarious situation in which I was now irrevocably embroiled.

I changed tactics. I told Wolf that it would hurt me forever if he jumped before my eyes; that I would never be the same again, that my life would be ruined, I would have post-traumatic shock, nightmares, be unable to live with myself knowing I should have tried to stop him. Perhaps that might matter to him, although why would it? I certainly felt it to be true.

'Well,' he said in a sober tone, 'why don't you just go on home then. I'll wait until your train is gone.' He thought that would make me go away. But, of course, it didn't.

'Mr Wolf,' I said, in what I hoped was a reasonable, practical tone of voice, anxious to keep my mounting desperation under wraps, 'the police are on their way. If there's a reason why you'd rather not see them, perhaps you should just go back up the stairs and leave now.'

'Who do you think I am?' he sputtered. 'I'm an honest man. I've done nothing to be ashamed of.' Now I had to apologize, make nice; I had offended him. It was exhausting. 'Oh God, I'm sorry,' I mumbled, 'just not sure what to do to keep you safe.'

Then I began to tell him about my life, not just to build some kind of rapport and manipulate him into changing his mind, but also because I was wound up and it was a relief. It poured out of me in a rush of pent up emotion, months in the making. It was now me who was in tears. I told him that since my husband had left, everything in the house had broken: the toilet; the garage door; the pot lights in the kitchen; the washing machine. I told him that my teenage daughter was only pretending to go to school and I had caught her with her boyfriend in bed; that we had a homeless kid living with us who was eating all our food; that I was lonely and no one was lining up to be with me. And that the one person who had actually been paid to help me navigate my new circumstances had thrown me out of her office. He listened carefully. He empathized. What a strange pair we were: me, a middle-aged, overweight, harried bureaucrat having a meltdown in the semi-light of the underground; and he, a shabby, sick, skinny fellow on the brink of a life-threatening decision. We bonded.

'Things will turn around for you in a bit, you'll see,' he said, wisely. 'They always do.'

'Do they?' I replied. 'For you too, do you think?' My words were not lost on him.

The minutes ticked by. There was no one else around but us. We were engaged in a deep mutual confidence. I heard more about his life, which had been good until the last few years. He heard some more about my separation, my whacked-out kid, my out of control domestic life, my financial troubles. I stopped worrying after an hour or so about whether he would jump. He was going nowhere.

We were jolted out of our bubble by loud, commanding voices, yelling, 'Don't move. Stay where you are.'

Hands pushed us apart, pinning Wolf forcibly against the wall. A policewoman asked me, 'Did he attack you? Are you alright? Do you need an ambulance?' They had it all wrong.

Two policemen, holding him tightly, marched him back up the stairs.

I screamed out, 'Don't hurt him. He needs medical help. He's a good man.' I didn't even have the chance to hug him goodbye, this stranger who had become so intimate.

I gave my name, phone number and a very brief description of what had happened. I put as good a face on it as I could muster.

Then I got on the next train. I was trembling throughout my entire body; the adrenaline had worn off.

No one was home. I remembered that it was her night with her dad. I had a double scotch with a splash of water, some toast and Marmite, watched *Coronation Street*, and went to bed. I told no one what had happened the next day because I had just started a new job. I didn't know too many people and I was the boss. Bosses don't confide in their staff in some workplaces, and this was one of those. So I pushed it to the back of my mind.

As time went by, I noticed little things that had begun to turn around in my turbulent life. I went on a couple of dates; I got a generous tax rebate; my work was challenging; the washing machine got fixed.

'Hah, an angel is on my shoulder,' I told my sister, laughing. 'Must be the magic of Mr Wolf.'

Late that August, I got a phone call from the police. Wolf had been taken to hospital that February night where he had recuperated. I was nominated for an award for heroism. I exhaled. Wolf was going to be fine, he would survive. And so, it seemed, would I.

Kindness is a language which the deaf can hear and the blind can see.

MARK TWAIN

A FULL HEART

Francesca White

I have had so many losses over my 60-plus years. My Italian father died in a tragic accident when I was 32; at the time I did not know I was pregnant with my second child, yet happiness was soon overshadowed when I suffered a miscarriage. To this day I still think of my dad, and I also wonder what my child would have been like. As the years pass I have come to the realization that it doesn't matter how old you are, some of life's experiences will still take a hold and cause heartache.

Not long before my Russian mother passed away, I found her sitting at her dining room table, silent tears flowing from her eyes.

I sat next to her, took her hand and asked, 'Mama, what's the matter?' She then recounted the story of the last moments of her dying little girl, how tightly the child held on to her finger. Mum had been at the bedside for hours. Not able to hold on any longer, she prised her young child's hand away from her and rushed to relieve herself.

'When I got back, Irena was gone. It was as if her holding on to my finger had kept her breathing.' Mum then began to sob. Something that had occurred well over 70 years ago was as fresh in her mind as if it had happened just yesterday.

So it is with me. I feel the losses as clearly, as vividly now even though so much time has passed. It increases whenever I lose something or someone else. Yet even when I was seriously ill with cancer I found the love to carry on. It would come in different forms. Some kind act from a nursing staff member or a friend. Thoughtful gifts, messages, hope. There is loss, there is also surviving loss, becoming stronger in many ways. During my illness, many people remarked on how 'calm' I was, while others commented on how 'strong' I seemed.

This was partly due to my spiritual beliefs. Laughter was also wonderfully therapeutic. Both my parents loved to laugh; they also enjoyed going out to places that made us all happy, whether it was the zoo, botanical gardens, the cinema or to the beach.

I often repeated a silent mantra particularly when I was ill: 'Patience, faith, perseverance.' The wise words 'One day at a time' are extremely helpful — when you think about it, it's all that we ever have.

I learnt a lot about living from my parents. Some years back I travelled to Albury to visit an old migrant camp in Bonegilla. It was a familiar feeling for me as I walked onto the grounds. I remembered my mother talking of the time when she first arrived in Australia and the name Bonegilla was often mentioned. As a child I never knew that Bonegilla was indeed what it was called. I had thought my Russian mother was mispronouncing it, as she often did, and it wasn't until many years later I discovered she was saying it correctly. Bonegilla was named by the local Aborigine folk; it is said to mean 'deep water hole'.

I grew up with a heavy load upon my young shoulders. It was like a burden of grief descended upon me, still clinging on as I grow older although not as strong as it used to be. Of course, it wasn't all tears and heartache; there were many joyous get-togethers when I was a child as my Italian and Russian relatives gathered to eat, drink, play music and sing. Celebrating the fact that now they all lived in a peaceful country, abundant with all the necessities of life plus a whole lot more.

However, at other times there were the late-night discussions, whispered secrets of places and people I had no knowledge of. I stood silently, hiding behind a curtain in the passageway of our small inner-city house listening to the true-life stories shared by my mother and some of her friends.

My mother's first husband was shot to death just 50 kilometres from the city of Kiev. It happened in a tiny Jewish village called Grebonkin, the final stage of a 700-kilometre walk from the Latvian city of Riga, where both Mum and her husband worked for a school. It was 1942, during World War II, and their two small children had both died from hunger and disease. It was decided they should make their way to Kiev where my grandmother lived. Since there was no available transport, the journey would be on foot.

The Germans came at night to Grebonkin. Mum's husband was rounded up with other Jewish males (most of whom lived in the village). The next morning the rest of the villagers were ordered to accompany the soldiers and prisoners to an open pit in the nearby woods. One by one the men were shot in the back of the head.

Mum remembered collapsing to the ground. The two Ukraine police working with the Germans began to drag her away. 'She can join her husband tomorrow, little Jewess,' they smirked to her face. An old man standing quietly in the crowd came forward and addressed the German captain. He knew a little of the German language. 'Sir, I know this young woman, we came from Riga, she is not a Jew, if you look closely she is wearing a cross around her neck. She has already lost her two children and now her husband; could she not be spared?'

Mum always recalled this moment in her life as the one that gave her hope in times of adversity. The old man and the German officer were compassionate. The officer was a victim of circumstance as they all were, someone who was more comfortable working in a bank rather than being in command of heartless individuals doing the devil's work. He ordered that no harm should come to my mother or any of the women or children in the village. And so it was that my mother escaped death on that fateful day to live on for a further 70 years in a land so far away.

I thought about this story as I wandered around the Bonegilla camp grounds, now being refurbished for the many migrants and their future relatives to re-visit, to remember, to give thanks for a brand new life. I came upon Block 19; one of these buildings housed my mother all those years ago. There were wonderful displays of photographs in a building nearby.

Tears of gratitude flowed down my cheeks as I thought of the struggles my parents had had, particularly my mother, even after arriving in this new country, a place where she would eventually die. Everything she had ever known was changed forever. Two years after my mother arrived, her mother and one surviving sister also migrated to Australia. These were the only relatives I ever knew on my mother's side.

Of course, being Russian did not make it easy for me growing up. I may have been born here, yet that did not deter the ignorant remarks of fellow school kids. Discrimination comes from a whole range of perceived differences and occurs in all eras. Postwar European migrants as well as their offspring, whether they were born overseas or not, were an easy target for misguided people. I also had my share of rude remarks from kids at high school when they saw my dad. He had a very dark complexion, with dark hair and eyes, while I was fair with blue eyes and blonde hair. Well, you can imagine some of the remarks I got — it was not pleasant at all.

I guess all these experiences gave me an incredibly tolerant and compassionate view when meeting with other nationalities, people who were different to me. I couldn't give a toss what a person looks like or what shape their eyes are; accents are nothing new to me; which religion they believe in; I couldn't care less, as long as a person is kind and friendly then I will get on with them. I knew what it was like to be given a label, to be put in a certain box as imagined by others.

I feel that it doesn't matter what year you are born, there will always be good and bad. I never give up hope — you never know what new discovery is just around the corner, what new medicines or new technology. The world evolves and so do its inhabitants. Just when I think I can't be amazed, something in nature will catch my attention, like the sun shining on droplets of water on a frosty morning, giving the impression that many diamonds are glittering on a tree or other surface. It's just magical. I love those moments, and I appreciate all I have in life.

How **beautiful** a day can be when kindness touches it!

GEORGE ELLISTON

THE INVISIBLE BRIDGE

Mark Lovell

Becoming an octogenarian doesn't happen all at once. Gradually, habits become ingrained. Self-sufficiency increases in importance, since anything undermining it suggests loss of control. The more that I trusted myself to do whatever I used to do previously without thinking, the more I tended to assume that continuity was there to stay. My wife and I are a strong team. Strong enough to believe in our strength.

This encouraged fostering the idea of being a separate unit. I began to regard our way of living as normal, desirable. Other, younger people were over there, almost out of sight. Without actually condemning them, I increasingly parcelled them up in a common stereotype: they were high on technology, low on social feelings and interaction. This sense of generation split made me unaware of the invisible bridge.

Suddenly, in the depths of a Montreal winter, my life took a dramatic turn. In a brief moment of inattention or over-confidence — possibly both — I stepped on black ice. This happened on a street corner in Montreal, close to the Atwater Market. I was carrying a bag in either hand, which meant I landed face foremost on an unforgiving sidewalk. I tried to get up, which seemed hard and painful. I looked around but my glasses had fallen and were now broken. So much for my self-sufficiency.

I heard young French voices nearby. A group of seven or eight men and women in their early twenties came close and I felt hands on my shoulders, starting to lift me up. I also became aware of rivulets of blood coursing from my face and onto my chest and arms. The voices above me argued briefly; they decided they should check my legs and ankles before lifting me to my feet. Satisfied that my lower body had no fractures, they brought me over to a nearby park bench.

'Watch out!' I gasped to them in French. 'There's blood everywhere.'

One of them thrust a bunch of tissues into my hand. With these I dabbed at my face, which was a painful act to accomplish. For themselves, they didn't seem to care. In fact, two of them sat very close to me, on either side, to help me keep warm. It was −15°C that afternoon.

'Watch out for your clothes!' I urged. 'Cleaning bills!'

'That doesn't matter at all,' one woman insisted. 'How are you feeling, sir?'

This began a discussion about where I was going. My self-sufficient side assumed I would soon stop bleeding, wipe my face, rest a bit, then pick up my bags and head home by subway.

My new friends smiled and shook their heads. They knew better. One of them was already on his cellphone, dialing 911. He paused, then asked me whether I wanted a particular hospital. Automatically I said Montreal General since that was the closest to home. I heard him say 'Trauma, *oui*,' into his phone. Then, to me: 'They'll take you to Montreal General.' He added that while most hospitals had an emergency section, not all dealt with trauma cases such as a fall.

The others wanted to know when the ambulance would arrive. He told them he'd been given an estimate of 15 minutes. My companions on the bench, my human bookends, each shifted closer to me, determined to keep the cold away until the ambulance came.

The French they used with me was slow and careful, very different from their rapid-fire chatter among themselves. Less comfortable in English, they made every effort in French to avoid misunderstandings between us.

Who were these people, I wondered? They were young, they gave an impression of being sports- or fitness-oriented. Students? Possibly, not necessarily. Surely they had better things to do than—

'Do you mind my asking, sir, are you married? Should we call your wife? Or perhaps your children?'

'Oh! Yes, of course. Thank you!' I gave them my wife's name and our home number.

He called but there was no answer so he left a message. Disappointed, he seemed to feel it might be his fault. 'Was that a landline? What's her cellphone number?' I shook my head despite the pain this caused. The irony here was that, yes, we had a cellphone but it was usually in the car, just for emergencies, and I couldn't remember the number. Young people's predilection for technology made more practical sense.

Once they decided to help me, they didn't want to let me go. An older man, thirties maybe, stopped by the bench and asked what was going on. He spoke with a European French accent and seemed eager to help. My team was very polite with him, thanking him but making it clear they were in control. 'The ambulance is on its way,' said one of them. 'We're staying here until it comes,' said another. I was in protective custody, which felt good.

Two of them kept me talking. One said she wasn't a Montrealer, she came from Trois Rivières. Did I know her town? Up to that moment, I'd thought of Three Rivers simply as something that happened on the North Shore route to Quebec City. That was all. I had to say more because my mind now flooded with respect for its inhabitants. '*Une très jolie ville*,' a very nice town, I managed. Okay, an invention, but necessity was its mother.

Another wanted to cheer me up. He found my glasses and waved the frame at me. One of the frame wings had come off. 'You could use it like this,' he suggested, imitating an elderly nineteenth-century lady with a lorgnette. We all laughed. I wished I could laugh more freely — like them — but it was painful because of the broken bones behind and around my nose.

One woman kept more to herself. She had taken on the role of the person who anticipates possible problems. 'Do you have your *carte soleil*?' she asked me. Yes, my Quebec health insurance card was in my wallet. She looked relieved, then went back to pondering. Soon after, 'Are you diabetic, sir?' Another look of relief when I answered no. Her kindness took the form of investigation.

How these people *blend*, I thought to myself. They have a common purpose. They assume roles, sometimes individual, sometimes not, but always in line with that purpose. Very different from the stereotype of 'me first' that is sometimes attached to Generation Z.

They examined my two shopping bags. One bag made suspicious sounds when picked up. 'Oh monsieur!', someone cried, '*Votre pot est cassé!*' They looked as if the breakage was their own tragedy — something bad happening to them.

I told them it must be the jar of buckwheat honey I'd just bought in Atwater Market.

'Olivier! You're the fastest.' The ambulance would be here soon, so the designated athlete was despatched. 'Watch out for the ice!' somebody shouted after him, but I doubt whether he heard it or cared. Olivier turned briefly to ask, 'Small or large?' The rest of the team shouted back to him, 'Large!' And 'Remember buckwheat!'

I tried to reach my pockets but my arms and shoulders were stiff and slow to accept orders. 'Please — look in my wallet for some money!'

'Oh no!' said the woman sitting next to me. 'Forget *that!*' It was almost as if I'd proposed a sacrilege.

A minute before the ambulance arrived there were two carrier bags in Olivier's hands — my old one containing vegetables, plus a clean new one containing a large pot of buckwheat honey protected by a sheath of crushed newspaper. He stood ready to load them on board once I was inside the ambulance.

While I was carefully picked up and fastened to a stretcher, I wanted to make a little thank you speech. All I could manage was *'Merci! Merci infiniment, tout le monde!'* They smiled but declared practically in unison, *'Oh non, monsieur! C'est normal.'*

They held a brief Q and A with the ambulance paramedics. Talking rapidly, Francophone to Francophone, they were hard to follow. But I understood they'd prepared a report on my condition. Confused? the paramedics asked. Not really, they were told. Shocked but lucid. Fell on his face: bleeding from nose, mouth and a cut above the eye. Hands bruised but not bleeding. Pain in head and neck. No analgesics given. Legs, ankles seem okay but stumbles. Most of this was contributed by the woman who had spent much of the time frowning, looking out for unforeseen difficulties. So this was what she had been quietly assembling.

'Bon voyage!' they all shouted as the ambulance doors closed. They were now back on their side of the invisible bridge, the connection of human kindness that remains largely unseen and unsuspected until actually needed. Once the bridge is summoned it becomes very obvious, linking contrasting generations and negating prejudice based on stereotypes.

Today's **mighty** oak
is just yesterday's nut,
that held its ground.

DAVID ICKE

DEAD MAN WALKING

Col Henry

I have heard the phrase many times before; usually uttered as a throwaway line in a movie or a book. A frowning threat of revenge from the western outlaw or some latter-day criminal … 'You're a dead man walking.' But the good guy was of strong character, a hero even, and usually came out the winner in the end. Right?

Until now, I have never really thought in any great depth about how most of us would feel under such a threat. Those who never in their wildest dreams would rate themselves as a 'hero'. Those small in stature or handicapped by some physical weakness, or with mental or emotional restraints.

To these people, 'You're a dead man walking' hits hard. For some it comes as a sudden shock. A disturbing realization that they are accepting the truth of it. For them, the dagger-like question springs forward … 'How much time do I have left?' In truth, the answer is the same for all us: we do not know.

I am 74, an old man now, so for me it must be less than for most of the younger ones. I can no longer run marathons, carry on all night or easily handle the stress of the hectic, multitasking of modern city life. My joints ache, I have lost a lot of my mobility and strength. Yup, I've had to slow down.

And therein lies the problem. No one seems to have time to share and meaningfully communicate any more. We communicate more by machines now than by the nourishment of face-to-face conversation.

I drive carefully, especially in bad conditions, but not too slow. I travel at or preferably just below the speed limit. I am constantly amazed at how many vehicles go zooming past me.

Last week I was driving at 60 kilometres per hour in a 60 zone. The booming thump of rap music drew my eyes to my rear-view mirror. A Subaru WRX had rapidly come from behind and was now tailgating my car. Up ahead I saw two women, one pushing a pram, about to start out on a marked pedestrian crossing. I lightly tapped on the brake several times to alert the driver behind and then braked steadily to stop for the women.

The WRX driver yanked his vehicle to the right, blasted on his air horns and ripped through the crossing. Fortunately, the blast of his horns brought the women to a sudden halt and no harm was done.

As fate would have it, the Subaru was stopped at the next red light. My driver's window was already down. I looked across at the two swarthy young men both wearing reversed baseball caps. The driver lowered the passenger side window. Their music was deafening, the bass vibrating through my body.

The grinning passenger shouted, 'Why don'tcha get outta the way, Grandpa?'

I called out, 'Why don't you slow down? There were people on the crossing back there!'

The driver replied, 'Fuck you!' and stuck up his middle finger. 'Ya stupid old c%#t. You're a dead man walking.'

The lights turned green. The WRX took off with a roaring exhaust and turbine howl. I noted the registration number but did not report the incident.

On that evening's TV news, I saw a rear view of that same car, with matching registration. It was shown impaled head-on into a tree in suburban Punchbowl.

The TV reporter stated:

... and the street has been closed off. Both front seat passengers were pronounced dead at the scene. The rear seat passenger, a fifteen-year-old male, suffered multiple injuries and was taken by ambulance to Bankstown Hospital where he remains in a critical condition.

A police spokesman said that investigations were underway at the scene. And that it seemed that no other vehicle was involved. He said that police believe the driver had lost control of the vehicle and that excessive speed may have been a contributing factor to the cause of the accident. Back to you Mike.

I was pleased that no other vehicle or pedestrians were involved. But I was shocked because, if only for a brief moment, I had met these men. I was not overly surprised at what had happened, but I drew no satisfaction from their deaths.

It is not an easy task to understand our fellow man. So many of us struggle to walk in our own shoes let alone walk in another's. We have no control over where or to whom we are born or how we look. But we will be who we become, and we become what we make of ourselves. We are unique individuals and we do not have to live up to the expectations of others. We all have our own dreams to aspire to and our own expectations in life.

It becomes much easier when we learn and accept that humans are our travelling companions. They should not be our natural enemies; not in our lives or on our roads. We must share our world and help each other.

So, who were these young men? Fit and well, they had so much to live for. Were their lives thrown away for cheap thrills?

Psychiatrists would inform us that the young men had a strong inferiority complex and were compensating with ongoing shows of power and superiority to gain recognition and acceptance in society. We would all agree their behaviour and attitude were foolish and ultimately self-destructive. It was a sad ending and the question follows ... Why?

It is difficult to realize that life is not a competition, that everyone at times is a winner or a loser. That we are all share a membership of humanity and we can all contribute to the success of the team. An entrenched inferiority complex can have us living in fear of exposure. It takes courage to be honest and true to ourselves and not to make a pretence of being superior.

We are all born with some measure of intelligence, but we are not born with wisdom. We live, and we learn. Some knowledge is forced upon us by discipline and schooling. Other things we learn from our awareness, observations and experience of life itself.

We acquire wisdom ourselves. Others may offer it to us, but it is not ours until we accept it. It is not an age thing. Wisdom can come to us through the words and actions of infants. It is not the knowledge itself but how we use it. Even when we do acquire wisdom we sometimes forget or simply do not use it in the best way.

Was I wrong to call for the driver to slow down? Was I being the wise old man trying to teach him a lesson? Was he in an angry mood for the rest of the day? In the afternoon did he use speed as an outlet resulting in the fatal accident?

I can still see them; the dead men walking.

There's no such thing as a small act of kindness. Every act creates a ripple with no logical end.

SCOTT ADAMS

UNDER THE LAW

Judy Light Ayyildiz

In 1963, West Virginia required six weeks of student teaching for receiving a BA in Music Education — my prized goal from Marshall University. It had already been a full year for me. I married in the late fall; and my dad disowned me for marrying a foreigner. But I turned 22 in February, and had made the choice to prove myself a strong, independent female.

By January, my husband had gotten a physician's surgical residency in a Huntington hospital. We would finally live in the same city. That meant an apartment to keep and extra cooking — on top of my senior voice recital in April, final instrument examinations, theses and tests, along with entertaining my hearty life-mate. I gave up my part-time job at Anderson-Newcomb department store.

By the end of March, an obstetrician confirmed my suspicions. Lucky for us, I proved healthy. My attitude continued to lean towards making do in order to achieve goals. I became absolutely thrilled with the idea of having a baby come November. I just had to graduate in May. Plus, there was my leading comic role in the spring production of *Brigadoon*, which I really wanted to do; and the mandatory student teaching that had been my dream for years.

Although we couldn't get over the wonder of being channels for the new life that was growing inside me, my husband agreed we had to keep it a secret until I graduated. I hoped that was possible. There were hurdles to be sure; but I was slender, so a few more pounds would only look like the contented flesh of marriage. Normally, physical activity came easily to me. So the musical's rehearsals and dancing and getting twirled overhead by a couple of males on stage would prove to be a breeze. No one need even know.

However, throughout the required six weeks of practice teaching, I would be breaking the state law. I wondered, would I be guilty of a felony or a misdemeanor? The stupid law most likely sprung from the hands of a bunch of holier-than-thou men who couldn't see that pregnant teachers were no different than pregnant mothers. For goodness sake! Young people had always witnessed obvious results of their parents' married behaviours. Yet siblings managed to keep sound minds and emotional balance after daily, routine revelation of Momma's big belly. Thus, I reasoned that it was fine to break a law that involved the most basic act of existence experienced by society. Most of the general public must have taken the same stance as me. A few years later, that state law was repealed. Young people today are aghast that such an idea ever stood. My hormones were outraged. During my student teaching, I meant to show how willpower helps the private choice prevail.

And so, I had my plans; but I hadn't realized that my student teaching would come in the middle of pregnancy's early nausea. The truth is, as a general rule, the 1950s generation knew next to nothing — fact-wise — about procreation. Polite people didn't even use the word 'pregnant'. Instead, folk said quietly, 'She's in *that* way.' My mother, with her eyes fixed and one red brow raised to underline the tone in her voice, called it 'P-R-E-G' — spelling out the four letters rather than saying the entire word.

Soon, the mystical *Brigadoon* danced into the past; and I stood before my student teacher supervisor Janice Chandler's choirs, with my arms upraised, podium in front of me, and solar plexus jumping threateningly with every crescendo.

I couldn't keep anything in my stomach. Sure, I used the mind to overcome a taxing situation, but this was like treading in choppy waves. My strawberry-blonde bob must have turned green and my freckles white while I repeatedly reminded myself, *Under no circumstances do you upchuck while on duty in the classroom.* Thinking the word 'vomit' made me sicker to my stomach. *Nor let on if you feel the slightest bit off.* The worst washed over me when the cafeteria exploded its morning glory scents down the hall about 10.30 a.m. The smells would last until after noon, hanging in the air like mouldy clouds. Again, I willed myself to ignore my body's reaction. Of course, I couldn't. But I continued in my mode. For years after, school cafeteria smells in the halls haunted my memory like meddlesome spooks.

I walked with Ms Chandler to the cafeteria, where we passed to the head of the jabbering line and slipped plastic trays along the metal bars that ran in front of the overcooked meatballs and macaroni. We would then talk blithely as we passed down the hall and up the stairs to the teachers' lounge — with me all the while silently picturing the bathrooms that were empty while students ate lunch. Naturally, I avoided being heard gagging in the teachers' lounge. The thought of a cold and empty stall meant relief. But first, I had to take my tray into the room, set it down, greet all those faces around the long table, and make some pleasant small talk. My behaviour was being monitored every moment by my mentor. When I excused myself after placing my tray, I hoped that the sly glances from those seated indicated mindful understandings that, after all, I was still a young bride — and that whatever it was that made me have to go into the privy so often during lunch somehow shouldn't be mentioned. When I returned, I'd nibble. Jell-O went down okay, as did the crackers and sometimes bread without butter. Meat was totally out, although I could fathom a few bites of the pinto beans as long as I added extra salt. 'No wonder you're so skinny. You never eat enough to feed a hummingbird,' was the sort of thing they said. I told them it was the stress of senior year; and they nodded, a bit bored.

I made it through the student teaching. A few weeks after that came graduation. I didn't graduate with honours, but I finished decently. Four years earlier, when we music freshmen had assembled all together that first semester, we'd been told that half of our 80 would be gone by January. Only eight of the 80 made it across the stage. I informed those eight that we were actually nine. It felt joyous. I could hardly believe my luck.

The day after commencement, I showed up at Janice Chandler's room during her free period. She looked up happily. 'Did you come to tell me you have graduated?'

'Yes! But I have something else to tell you, a surprise.'

Her blue eyes twinkled. 'What, that you're pregnant?' She had used the word. I stopped in my tracks.

Janice got up and came to me. She placed her hands on the top of my shoulders and studied my face. 'Honey, I told myself, six weeks ago, "That girl is pregnant."'

'But you never let on.'

'I couldn't,' she sighed. 'You were so sick and yet you did everything I required you to do without complaining. I told myself that if you can get through it without talking about it, then I don't have to acknowledge it.'

'How did I give myself away?'

'Oh, honey, I've got my own kids. But if you had said anything about it, I would have been obliged to report it, under law. You didn't. I didn't.' She stepped back. We grinned at each other.

What Janice did for me was one of the best acts of human kindness I could imagine. Without my degree, I might have never taught. That I was instilled with the idea that I was always meant to be a teacher required, at certain times, a guiding hand that lifted beyond my will or plans.

Kindness
makes a fellow
feel good
whether it's
being done to
him or by him.

FRANK A. CLARK

BOB

Dale Lorna Jacobsen

For years I had dodged him. He had always irritated me, the way he would never finish a sentence, just give a hint of the word he was seeking in the hope that someone would find it for him: 'You know that harp player … Nar … Mar …'

I knew the harp player's name, but let him struggle. I wasn't his keeper. Then I felt pity for this old man in front of me.

'You mean Marelle?'

'Yeah. That's it. Narelle.'

He's a hopeless case, I thought.

I was the only woman among a group of luthiers at the Queensland Timber and Working with Wood Show, there to display our handcrafted musical instruments. At lunchtime, I escaped to the exhibitor's lounge away from the incessant white noise: the whine of routers; the clanging of steel rims being hammered into place by a cooper; barracking crowds at the cross-cut saw race. It wasn't much quieter in the lounge, but the 2-metre high partitions dampened the din a little.

Too late, I saw him at one of the tables. He smiled and pulled an empty chair out for me to join him for lunch. I looked around, but there was no escape. It would have been too obvious if I sat at another table. I made some inane comment like, 'It's a bit quieter in here'. He noisily slurped from his Styrofoam cup, then wiped the beads of moisture from his scruffy beard with the back of his hand. He leaned close to me, conspiratorially.

'You know, I'm an old lefty.'

Now, this came as something of a surprise. I hadn't been aware he had political leanings.

'Really?'

'Yeah. I'm an old fart now, but in me days, I used to go to all the demos.'

I struggled with the image; looked closer at him. *Mmm ... perhaps it's possible.*

It appeared that the rest of the blokes had been talking about me behind my back, discussing my new path in life — writing. Most of them knew I was writing a novel about my unionist grandfather. Obviously, word had spread to Bob.

'You remember when Fred whatsit got hit on the head?'

There was only one person he could have been talking about: Fred Paterson, barrister, and the only member of the Communist Party of Australia to have been elected to parliament in 1944. Before my time.

'Fred Paterson?'

'Yeah, that's him. I was there, you know. I picked up his hat and dusted it off for him. Some bloke told me to rack off. Geez, he was a big bugger too. I told him to mind his own business, then he came at me. I'm not short, but I never had much meat on me so I bent me head forward and rammed it into his ribs as he got to me, and then grabbed him by the goolies ...' His hand cupped upwards in demonstration.

I was dumbfounded. This self-deprecating man would never swear in front of man or woman without mumbling 'pardon the language', but for the next half an hour he rolled off story after story — funny ones, poignant ones, stirring ones — oblivious to the saliva that sprayed with his enthusiasm.

He'd been in so many workshops, worked on the wharves, done many things in his long life and yet for years I had considered him pretty much a waste of space.

The next day he arrived half an hour after I did, and before he put down his carry bag, he plunged his hand in and withdrew two books.

'Thought you might like to have a look at these.'

Two treasures: a first edition of the Frank Hardy novel *Power Without Glory*, all tattered from being read so many times, and a small booklet damning the Queensland coal mining industry during the era of Premier Bjelke Petersen.

'Hey, thanks Bob. Can I borrow them?' He shuffled uneasily.

'I don't lend books. Too precious. You can look at them here, today.'

I felt embarrassed at having asked such a favour, and spent the whole day with my head buried in the precious books.

Come lunch time, there he was again, same table, pulling out the chair for me to join him. This time I wanted to. I wanted to hear more of his stories.

'By crikies, you've stirred me up. I didn't get to bed till two this morning. Me and the missus sat up going through the bookcase. I thought I was past it all, but it's come bubbling to the surface. Good on you girlie! I'm not trying to convert you, mind, but you got to know what it was like from the inside if you're gonna write this stuff.'

'That's okay,' I smiled. 'I'm already converted.'

Again the stories flowed. The strikes, the jargon. All gold to the ears of a writer. I itched to reach for my pen and notepad, to take notes so as not to miss anything, but I knew this wasn't the time and place. I just listened, ears strained above the machinery noise that was too loud, and absorbed the whole like a sponge, confident I would be able to recall his words when needed.

At the end of lunch, Bob carefully picked up a green plastic bag that had been lying between us on the table and pulled out a large red-covered book entitled *Time of Conflict*. I opened it and read the inside jacket: 'A novel by Judah Waten'. I knew of this author who, despite being Russian-born, held a mirror to Australian society. I began to read: 'When young Mick Anderson slipped from home in the early morning to help his digger father steal sheep …' I wanted to keep reading. I doubted I would be able to borrow this from a library. It was too old.

'You can spend the day skimming through it,' said Bob.

I looked up at him, unable to hide the fact that I coveted this book. He shuffled in his seat, fighting with himself over the decision he was about to make.

'Aw geez, I've never done this before, and I'll probably hate myself for it, but …' there was a very long pause, 'you can borrow it.' He got up from the table.

'Are you sure?' Silly question.

'Yeah, I reckon we've got the measure of each other. But I'll tell you, if you let me down ...' and he drew his finger across his throat.

'Oh, I promise, I won't let you down.'

For the rest of the week the other blokes looked at me, huddled in a corner with Bob, intently listening to what he had to tell me; my head ached from straining to catch every word above the din that bounced off the concrete walls and tin roof of the Show Pavilion. They knew I had always tried to dodge him. I could tell they were puzzled as to why I would prefer his company to theirs.

'Some people act real funny all of a sudden,' I overheard one of them say, nodding his head in my direction.

Never travel
faster than your
guardian
angel can fly.

MOTHER TERESA

AN ARCHIVE OF (A MEDICAL) CHILDHOOD

Rashida Murphy

I was not a healthy child. I was prone to accidents and ailments. Everything from jaundice and whooping cough to annual bouts of malaria. This on top of the flu, tummy bugs, nits, schoolyard mishaps, fractured limbs and other seemingly normal childhood rites of passage. I must have caused my parents such concern because I remember their puzzled frowns as they waited with me at various clinics or sat beside my childhood bed with prayer beads and flannel cloths.

But the 'sick child' morphed into an astonishingly healthy adult. And I've always been grateful for those early malaises, which seemed compensated for by healthy adulthood.

My parents took me to a legion of doctors every time something went wrong. Naturally, in small-town India, where my parents were well known, most doctors were also family friends. I was therefore obliged to call them 'Uncle' or 'Aunty' and they treated me with the avuncular jollity of impatient relatives. I don't think I ever went to a doctor I did not also know socially. Later, as a teenager, this became awkward, as I fell in love with a doctor's younger brother. I was never sure if the sanctity of the Hippocratic

Oath survived when families got together in the evenings and conversations went something like, 'That girl I saw this morning — wait, aren't you going out with her?'

However, apart from falling in love with my doctor's brother and then acquiring every known symptom that necessitated home visits, I was also regularly taken to see the ear, nose and throat specialist. He was a cheerful man with a carrying voice who called my father 'Ung-kill' in a loud, hearty tone laced with suppressed laughter. He would wave me towards a red vinyl swivel chair that tilted back alarmingly when he leaned over and asked me to open my mouth wide. He never stopped talking and laughing throughout the examinations, even when I had diphtheria, whooping cough, glue ear and conjunctivitis. He took each ailment in his stride, cheerfully explaining what I needed to do as if I was capable of managing my own health. My worried parents made him repeat everything he'd said to me and he'd wink at me and slap my father on his back and tell him I knew what to do. As far as I remember he never prescribed antibiotics, preferring to let nature run its course, believing in my body's ability to combat illness far more than I did. My mother inevitably sought a second opinion and pharmaceuticals for my rampant and unexpected illnesses. This ENT specialist whose voice and laughter still resonates in my memory was also a philanthropist and one of the earliest surgeons in my hometown to perform surgery for oral cancers. When someone couldn't afford the treatment he worked gratis. I have no idea how he made any money because he didn't charge people he knew, either, which was half the town.

None of the other doctors were shy about accepting a fee for their consultations and home visits. I think my father became an enthusiastic homeopath around this time, thinking he might save money by curing me with flower essences. And for a very long time Dad experimented with sugared pills and solutions smelling faintly of alcohol, with names like calendula and belladonna, and I became his favourite guinea pig. He perfected the art of quackery with me and by default became the preferred provider for a host of people who were naturally suspicious of doctors and clinics. To this day he continues to have a medicine cabinet filled with an array of bottles and tinctures. On my visits back to India, he explains the workings of various flowers and plants and retains a curiosity for healing my long-past illnesses. For his own needs, though, he relies on 'real' doctors. My mother reminds him of the time he thought he could fix a broken bone (mine) with flower essences and he pretends not to hear.

I fractured my left arm on a Sunday and, even though she denies it now, my mother's saintly patience finally snapped. It was the first time I remember her yelling at me when I was so obviously wounded and in pain. She had been cooking all day for the family of interstate cousins and aunties and uncles who were coming to dinner. And I turned up after a morning bicycle ride, with my clothes torn, blood on my knees and an arm hanging at an awkward angle. Mum lost it in several ways she chooses not to remember, but when she calmed down, she called our favourite doctor — the 'Ung-kill' man, otherwise known as Dr Khan.

With his usual bluntness, Dr Khan recommended I put up with the inconvenience for a day and go to the town's only orthopaedic surgeon on Monday. The alternative, he asserted, was to go to the bonesetter, and he wouldn't send any child of his to that man. I was dizzy with pain by this stage and Mum decided the bonesetter would do.

And so in the late afternoon light, my arm was tugged and pulled and stretched and my sister recalls fainting just watching me. I woke up in a dark room with my arm in plaster and a short man in a doctor's coat shouting at a woman in a nurse's uniform. Mr and Mrs Bonesetter, obviously. As it was Sunday evening, my family were busy with the delayed meal they would have had in the middle of the day, had I not chosen to ruin it in such a spectacular way. I cried and the people in the room turned to me, told me to shut up, and went back to arguing with each other. I lay there looking out through dusty louvred windows as the world darkened and I thought I had finally used up my family's goodwill.

When Dr Khan came to see me the next day, along with my sheepish family, he patted my head and told me I was lucky I could still function with my right arm. Turning to my father he said, 'Ung-kill, you have ruined the child's life. Who will marry her now? I told you not to go to the bone-breaker.' Dad laughed uneasily while Mum and I clutched each other in horror. They took me home and the next twelve weeks were the worst of my life. When the plaster came off, my arm was a bit withered and thin, but otherwise fine. Within a month I was back at Dr Khan's clinic with a chest infection and he pumped my left arm back and forth and announced that it was my good fortune rather than the bonesetter's skill that had ensured my healing.

Then I grew up, left home, became a healthy adult and raised my own daughter in a city so far from the one I grew up in that I didn't have a language to describe my childhood to her. Now as I confront my mortality in the form of a cancer diagnosis, so many years after those childhood mishaps, I am grateful for all those people who hobbled me back together after my reckless rides and fiery fevers. The voices, remedies, admonitions and concerns of family and health professionals still prompt me from time to time as I negotiate this new reality. I am fallible. Life is unsafe. But I'm still here, for now.

Honesty is the first chapter in the book of wisdom.

THOMAS JEFFERSON

DEAR JOHNNY J.

Bill Lennox

My mother sent me a clipping from the *Otago Daily Times* a few years ago. It reported that you were the new principal of a school in Central Otago. Well, I'm relieved the government has made corporal punishment illegal in New Zealand schools. Otherwise, a school in Central Otago was in for a bloodbath.

You see, the clipping reminded me of two things. Firstly, I remembered you being my Standard 4 teacher at primary school. Secondly, I remembered that I intended to write to thank you for making me a better person, especially a better teacher.

The classroom at my primary school was on the second level. It wasn't a multistorey school but it stepped up a hillside, so it was on three levels. Our Standard 4 classroom was at the top of the stairs and I remember it for two reasons.

Firstly, it was right beside a big landing where my friend Alan and I built a model landscape — it was actually just painted papier mâché hills with roads and cars. We made it for the school fair, though I can't imagine how we made any money out of it. We put all our Micromodel cars on it. Alan had a lot more than me because his father was a manager at the department store where we bought our Micromodels. My father worked on a road construction gang so I suppose we were the ideal pair for making a model landscape with roads and cars.

Come to think of it, that might have been why, for the next six years, I wanted to be a civil engineer. Then I decided to be an English teacher. I remember the moment I broke the news to my sixth form English teacher, Mary H. She threw her hands in the air and dragged me to the bookroom where she threw lots of books at me and told me to get studying right away. The problem was that I was in an Engineering class for whom academic English was not a priority. I've still got my well-thumbed copy of Oliphant's *A General Certificate English Course*. Hastily inscribed on the fly is 'William Lennox. Own copy. MH'.

The only detail I remember of the Standard 4 model landscape is a roadside hoarding we made out of cardboard. It advertised a car called the 'Rolls Canardly — rolls down hills and can 'ardly get up the other side'. We thought it was hilarious. I should have realized right there that I was more interested in words than engineering.

But you, Mr J. were one of the few teachers I had who inspired me to be a teacher. We called you (among ourselves) 'Johnny'. Even our parents did. It was a cool name back then, in the 1950s. There was Johnny Ray, Johnny Mathis, Johnny Mercer and Johnny B. Goode and our parents knew the words to *Frankie and Johnny* because Tex Morton sang it on the radio every single Sunday. There was something vibrant and energetic about the name Johnny, but it was also a bit tragic. So it suited you. You were quite handsome with your slicked back hair and your flashing smile, but you had a terrible temper.

I've had plenty of other teachers who got angry, but they usually found ways to redirect or suppress their frustration after too many hours with kids who wanted to be somewhere else. (Except Whacker Brown, who once caned half of our Physics class, but he was too young to know better. Anyway, we know he got ticked off later by the deputy principal.)

We always knew when some teachers were at the end of their respective tethers. An English teacher called Ernie J. would read Shakespeare flamboyantly all period, which I loved. Our maths teacher, Bill W. just clamped his jaw — the rippling muscle from jaw to temple was a sure sign. Another maths teacher, Eric H. had a nasal voice that would soar to a crystal-shattering pitch, and Oz A. would sulk at his desk until he dozed off.

My favourite teacher was Denis D. He was fun when he was riled — he imposed ridiculous penalties then mocked them. He once told me to stand with my nose touching the light switch then promptly told me off: 'Lennox! Stop being silly! You look ridiculous. Sit down!'

In fact, Denis D.'s parody of the tough teacher became another influence when I became a teacher. I recall confiscating a comic from a student and taking it into the back room where I loudly ripped up a whole newspaper. I gave the intact comic back to the student at the end of the lesson, saying something like, 'You can have this. I've read it.' In fact, I only remember that incident because I met the student years later and he told me about it, one of the few things he remembered from being in my class.

But you, Johnny J., alerted me to my own erratic emotions and motivated me to control them — and to have nothing to do with corporal punishment. In my first school, an all-male establishment in the 1970s where caning was rampant, I was the only teacher who didn't cane. Instead I somehow instilled a tone of mutual respect. It wasn't hard. I think it helped that I told them from the outset that I didn't believe in corporal punishment. I want to thank you for that too, Johnny J.

But I realize you probably don't remember the crucial occasion that launched me on this enlightened path, the second reason I remember our Standard 4 classroom at the top of the stairs.

I have no memory of the incident, but we must have been guilty of dire and malicious behaviour because eight of us found ourselves standing at the front the room being strapped. I guess the fact that I can't recall the offence discredits whatever warped behaviourist theory that once allowed bad tempered men like you to beat children.

Anyway, I do recall that I was last in the line-up of eight boys. Those before me got two of your quite vigorous whacks on their palms. That exertion didn't diminish your energy, but it did impair your reason. You turned to me.

'And you Billy Lennox — you should have known better,' you said. And gave me four whacks.

I remember thinking at the time there was something wrong about that. Hadn't I read about judges giving shorter sentences for first offenders? What happened to time off for good behaviour?

I've been pretty hot on avoiding injustices ever since.
So thanks Johnny J. Bastard.

Beginning today, treat everyone you meet as if they were going to be dead by midnight. Extend to them all the care, kindness and understanding you can muster, and do it with no thought of any reward. Your life will never be the same again.

OG MANDINO

JOSHUA

Meg Freeman

'Why don't you sell up and move to the Cape, Mom, be nearer to us — get out of that crime ridden place? The girls will soon be starting school — you're missing so much of their growing up years.'

'We've been through this before Greta dear. Dad and I have been here 30 years, your dad has three more years to retirement, he's happy in his job and I'm needed at the clinic. Of course, we're thinking about it for our retirement but, financially speaking, we must see the next three years out. In the meantime, Dad has raised the wall and put razor wire on top — we strengthened the security gate and fitted another in the passage between the lounge and bedroom. So you see, we're quite safe.'

'You're so barred in that if there was a fire you wouldn't be able to get out. Oh Mom, it worries me to think of you two squashed between two high-rise buildings, blocked off from sun during the day and all that noise at night. If you moved down here you would have sea breezes and a view of the ocean.'

❋

Don't wear jewellery in Hillbrow, especially not gold chains — they'll be ripped off your neck in an instant. If you need to check the time, one of those cheap watches from the street vendors will suffice; the street vendors sell everything, from vegetables to videos. They're the Informal Sector.

Don't carry cash or a handbag — the bag snatchers loiter in the streets just waiting. If you want to see bags being snatched take the bus; from that vantage point it's like watching a sideshow. Don't tuck your cash in your bra either, it's not safe. In a flash they'll wobble your boobs and grab it. If you have to carry cash, put it in your shoes.

Hillbrow never sleeps. It throbs 24/7 to its own drumbeat of burglaries, murders, drugs, rape and the tune of police sirens ...

And where in the world would you find Hillbrow? Well, I'll tell you. It's a tiny 1-kilometre square suburb within walking distance of Johannesburg, that City of Gold in *Souf Efrika* that grew in the gold rush days of the 1890s from a dustbowl of tents and prefabricated dwellings to a city in less than ten years. A place that, it was predicted, would become a ghost town when the gold ran out. But it didn't and the tent village turned into a city. Folks with their newly acquired wealth left the dustbowl and moved up onto the brow of the hill and built themselves modern homes with verandas in the front and stables at the back.

In the century that followed, most of those homes were demolished to make way for the high-rise suburb it is today, a mini Hong Kong, cramming humanity together as never before, thus making it a haven for crime of every description. It's also the gateway and hideaway for migrants crossing the borders illegally.

Beneath all the mayhem of existence, there is always something to touch the heart, a human story, and as Blanche returned from the clinic late one afternoon, carrying two plastic bags, which were digging into her fingers, she heard what sounded like a kitten mewing. She stopped in her tracks and glanced around — she was only 30 metres from her home and the packets were really hurting, but she put them down and walked a few paces to the alleyway from where the sound was coming. She opened a rubbish bin and was convulsed by the stench and filth that she beheld, but there, wrapped in a torn rag was a newborn infant.

'Oh my God,' was all Blanche could utter.

With the baby under her right arm and the plastic bags in her left, she made it to her front door.

'What in heaven's name have you got there?' asked a flabbergasted George, who was relaxing with his evening paper.

'A baby,' was all Blanche could utter as she dumped the packages down and hastily made her way to the bathroom to bathe the infant, who was still sticky with afterbirth.

George saved the groceries and returned to his chair. He knew the full story would flow out soon enough.

Blanche returned with the bundle wrapped in a clean towel, which she placed on the sofa, then busied herself in the kitchen for a moment or two and returned with a cup.

'George, please go and scrub your hands thoroughly, I mean thoroughly and when you return I want you to hold this infant, dip your little finger into the cup of sugar water and let it suck your finger. I'm going to the chemist on the corner to buy some baby food.'

'What?' George was dumbfounded at his wife's request.

He dutifully scrubbed his hands but it was another matter to sit there with a newborn baby too exhausted to cry, and try to console it with sugar water from his baby finger. What would the hardened mechanics from the garage say if they saw him?

'Well little fellow,' said George soothingly, 'you've had a bad start to life — what a horrid world you've come into.'

He felt it important to communicate with the wee bundle in his arms. The whimpering had stopped and the infant's tongue was firmly wrapped around his little finger.

'Of course you're hungry but let go, I have to get more sugar water. Besides, I think we ought to be formally introduced ... I'm George and that good lady who found you is Blanche. She'll soon be back with something more substantial to fill the void in that little tummy, but what shall we call you — something good and strong I think. How about Joshua? That sounds like a strong, manly name.'

It seemed an age before Blanche came through the front door carrying a large package.

'And not before time — this little fellow has almost eaten my whole finger.'

'I came as quickly as I could. You seem to have managed in my absence.'

'Oh, Josh and I are good friends. He's been complaining about the delay in the main course, but the liquid refreshment went down a treat.'

'Oh good, give me just a moment to sterilize this bottle and make him a feed.'

'Where he's just come from, I doubt that bottle needs sterilization — just rinse it with boiling water and bring on the dinner.'

'Of course I'll report him to the child welfare, George — tomorrow, first thing — they'll know what to do.'

❖

'Thank you Mrs Reid for all you have done in this matter. We will be in touch as soon as possible.'

Two weeks became three and three weeks became four.

'Thank you for calling, Mrs Reid, but could you bear with us for just a little longer — the matter is being processed.'

'If the majority of the population does not come forward to foster abandoned babies, what happens to them?' Greta asked. She was appalled at what her mother had taken on and was phoning every day.

'Who knows, probably remain in institutions until they are old enough to go onto the streets to follow a life of crime ... my concern at this moment is that Joshua's tests have come back positive — HIV positive.'

'I get so mad to think that some irresponsible female out there with AIDS, who is prepared to dump her infant in a bin, is probably at this moment getting pregnant again,' said Greta. 'They should be rounded up and sterilized.'

'Yes, my dear, I share your sentiment, but what can I do about it? The reality of the matter is that Joshie is here in my home, getting fatter by the day, looking at us with two big eyes and smiling such a beguiling smile that even you would melt.'

'Mom you're getting soft. You're too old to take on such a responsibility.'

'I know, my love, and for sure the matter will be resolved. In the meantime, Josh goes to the clinic with me and they have agreed to donate towards his food and diapers and the Church has donated a cot and pram, so he no longer sleeps on the spare bed.'

'Mom, this sounds as though it's becoming permanent.'

'Not at all, my sweetie. I've been assured that the matter will be resolved shortly.'

❧

'Mrs Reid, you have had Joshua for six months now — and still I'm no further in finding a permanent home for him. I have a proposition to put to you. Please take your time to consider what I have to say. If you are prepared to foster Joshua in a formal way on a permanent basis, you will qualify for assistance. As things stand at the moment, I cannot find a home for him and I don't have the authority to compensate you unless you sign these forms.'

And so Joshua became a permanent member of the Reid family.

❃

'Oh George, you look as though you had a heavy day at work. Sit down and I'll get you a beer; and by the way, I've got good news. Joshie took his first step today … What's the matter George, you look quite queer.'

'Take a step outside for a moment, Blanche, there's something you should see. I found it by the front gate. It came with this note.'

'Pleez Missie, tek my beby. God will bles you.'

The Reids (names have been changed) remained living in their home in Hillbrow, Johannesburg, and fostered four babies, all testing HIV positive, before a receiving depot for AIDS babies was established.

People don't notice
whether it's winter
or summer when
they're happy.

ANTON CHEKHOV

LULLABY

Garrick Batten

'Right you lot, bed time!'

'Aw, Mum, not yet,' from the eight-year-old twins. They always did everything together.

'Can't we stay up later Mum? It's the holidays,' called Tim with ten-year-old child logic.

'Me too,' from six-year-old Lucy.

'Read us a story — yes, yes, a story,' they chorused.

This single mother, running out of patience at the end of school holidays was exhausted, with exasperation starting to boil. Four days of rain had drowned outside holiday activities, six-year-olds couldn't play Monopoly and the twins now scorned slap and snap card games. Tim just wanted his PlayStation despite his mother's concern at overexposure. Now her recently widowed father had come to stay, and she hadn't even had time to wash her hair.

'No time for stories. I've got all this wet washing and loads of ironing to do. Off to bed with you all. Now!'

'Can I help love?' offered her father.

'Oh Dad … please.' Father–daughter bonds planted in the womb had grown over the years of teenage tantrums, varsity hijinks, marriage in another country and now divorce. The Clyde family had always stood together.

'Yes tell us a story Grandpa.'

'Yes a story — please,' pleaded the twins together.

'Where will I start?'

'Tell us about when you were a little boy, but not too little,' suggested Tim, hoping for some tips on growing up. 'Did you like school? I don't. It's boring.'

'Yes boring,' said the twins.

'Do you want a story or not?' asked their grandfather. 'If so, come and sit by me on the couch — you Tim on the floor. But you've got to promise. Straight off to bed after I've finished.'

'Cross my fingers, look straight in the eye, break the promise and have to die,' they all chanted.

'Well, sit up here. All comfortable? Lucy, you can sit on my lap.' His bearlike arms wrapped her, and the twins crammed together like a packet of biscuits. Always together.

'Grandpa, you smell funny.'

'Lucy,' called her mother. 'That's very rude. Say sorry to your grandpa. He loves his pipe.'

'Sorry Grandpa,' she said, her mouth drooping.

'Smoking's bad for you — our teacher told us,' said the twins.

'*Children!* Your grandfather's trying to tell you a story. Listen, or off to bed.' Mothers have magical ears.

'Alright, listening? Now in Standard 6 we had gangs. Everyone was in a gang. All the boys anyway — not girls. They were too bossy.'

'What's Standard 6?' asked the twins

'That's like Year 8,' called out their mother from the ironing board.

'Did you have patches like the Mongrel Mob?' asked Tim.

'No, but we had gang names. There were three gangs in our class with kids from all round the district. When I first started school we had to get up early for the bus — just after seven every morning and didn't get home until after five. It was the mail van, actually, that went around to all the farms in our district. We just jammed in but at least it was warm when there was ice on the puddles. And the windows kept frosting over.'

'But what about the gangs?'

'Yes the gangs. Tell us about the gangs.'

Lucy didn't really understand about gangs but still joined in. 'Please Grandpa,' she pleaded.

'Well … yes … three gangs … I'm trying to remember … it was a long time ago.'

'You said that already Grandpa,' the twins chorused, but he looked hard at them. He coughed, hoicked and swallowed.

'I still remember them, mostly. The M and M gang — all their names started with M. There was Mick, Max, Mac — he was really Allan MacIntosh — then Mark, Miles and Monty.'

'We had a puppy called Monty once,' interrupted Tim, 'but he got run over.'

'Well I don't think you should have any dogs in the city. Farms're the only place for dogs. I had five dogs on the farm when I retired. We couldn't have farmed without them. I had Flo and

Butch and Rock … can't remember the others right now. I still miss them. You could cuddle up to them on a very cold day on the hill. I remember one day …' But Tim interrupted.

'Tell us about the gangs Grandpa.'

'Well,' he battled on, smiling to himself, remembering. 'One gang had funny nicknames. They called themselves the Nicks. There were nine of them. I think I can remember. Spud Murphy and Dusty Miller. Then Snow White and Darkie Brown. I remember him — he was much fatter than anyone else. And Shorty Robinson, who was tiny. But they also had Tiny Timlake and he was actually tall.'

'Why was he called tiny if he was tall?' puzzled the twins with female logic.

'I don't know. Anyway, that wasn't my gang. Then the others were Lefty Latimer and Sandy Beach.'

'But you said nine,' accused Lucy. She clearly wasn't going to sleep.

'You must have been counting on your fingers — were you?'

'I can count up to a hundred, and I'm only six.' She snuggled down again. It wasn't easy keeping a place as the youngest of four, especially when the twins always worked together on everything.

'I can't remember the last one … it was Blue something.'

'Tim! Stop picking your nose,' came from the kitchen. 'What was your gang, Dad?'

'There were six of us and we had nicknames too, but we were much cleverer because our names really matched us. Well we thought so anyway, and our gang was the Animals. There was Fish Salmon, Jonah Williams — well, he looked just like a whale.

Do you learn about Jonah and the whale at Sunday school?' They nodded.

'Then Rudolph Hoffman ...'

'I know I know — Rudolph the red-nosed reindeer,' crowed Lucy. 'Did he have a red nose?'

'Lucy ... Lucy ... let your grandpa tell his story or I'll carry you off to bed.'

'We had Wuff O'Leary — he could make all sorts of barking and howling noises just like a dog. And Bull Gates — a big Māori boy — a bit older than us really, but a really great fellow.'

'What was your name, Grandpa?'

'I was called Neddy. Well, that was sort of from my name — Edward. But mostly because I came from a farm and had a horse of my own. And Neddy was a popular name for a horse.'

'Why did you have a horse Grandpa?'

'Later on, when we moved closer to town, I was allowed to ride to school. No, Tim, not a bike. My own pony. He was called Gerald, and my young sister used to double up with me. No saddle. Just a big sheepskin. There was a horse paddock at school, and some other kids rode, too. No one else in my class though.

'All farmers had horses in those days. We needed them to do the work. My father — your great grandfather — had a team. There were six of them. Big Clydesdales.'

'Ah! I get it,' cried Tim. 'Named after our family. Clyde.' He cast a superior glance up at the twins. 'Why didn't you have a tractor?'

'Well it was before tractors. And horses were great. They could go anywhere. They didn't get stuck. They stopped when you said, and they didn't have a lot of things go wrong if you looked after them properly. Fed them. And they all had names too — they were like friends. You could talk to them. They sort of talked back. You could understand them; well, my dad could anyway. And I could never really understand tractors.

'All the animals on our farm had names. Us kids were allowed to name the calves with girls' names. They started with the same letter but a different one each year so that you knew their age from the letter in the alphabet. We were up to G by the time I got a turn. I remember one year we ran out of names starting with L so one cow got called Lawrence.' The twins giggled sleepily. 'And a bull called Horace. A nasty Jersey bull. Us kids weren't allowed to go into his paddock by the house.'

He was interrupted by Lucy flopping onto one arm fast asleep. Obviously she'd lost interest in the story, or the warm ironing smell from the kitchen was too comforting.

'Come on now, you others. That's the end of the story. Off to bed. You promised. Remember?'

'I'm going to be in a gang,' said Tim.

'Us too,' called the twins.

'You're too young,' was Tim's scathing response.

'Come on — teeth then bed,' their mother called from the kitchen. 'Quickly now, you've had your story.' The children all uncurled.

'Thanks Dad, you're wonderful — a saviour. You've always looked after me. I never knew about your gang, though. Did you ever wonder what happened to all the others?'

'Probably like me, making up tall tales for their grandchildren to spare their mother.'

Too often we underestimate the power of a touch, a smile, a kind word, a listening ear, an honest compliment, or the smallest act of caring, all of which have the potential to turn a life around.

LEO BUSCAGLIA

THE OTHER MAN

Pamella Laird

He closed the heavy, studded door that led into the church. Mimicking his dejection, the dull thud echoed from pillar to pillar. Then silence.

The world had vanished as if he had entered another dimension. Pedestrian buzzer, car engines, exhaust-spewing buses and occasional laughter had always added reality to his life. But that reality was gone. The chatter of sparrows in the porch rafters had more meaning.

The walls held the serenity in their arms as if it were a treasure. Ken Mason hesitated, cautious, alone, haunted by the loss that had shattered his life. The world had moved on, leaving an airlock of thought to skulk in his brain like a malevolent fungus.

As far as he could see, in, around and beyond the shining brass lectern, no one else was in the building. He reached for the back of the nearest pew and, guided by its solidity, stumbled towards a side aisle. The deeply recessed windows of stained glass glowed like jewels in the late sun. The alien place smelled of snuffed candles and fusty tapestry kneelers.

Ken crouched forward on a polished seat, elbows on thighs, head in hands. He stared at his shoes; if the rest of his life was to be continued anguish, then in consideration of his own dignity, his shoes would always be shining. No one should ever think he was a 'down and out'.

The last of the sun gleamed through the round west window. Half turning, he noticed a kaleidoscope of colour on the carpet. A stream of floating dust motes drifted over his shoulder on to the empty seat beside him. Time passed while his mind, like an old film, replayed the hell of previous months.

His body and shoulders slumped. Finally, as the church grew dimmer, a sense of drowsiness, something close to calm, washed over him; the first taste of peace he could remember for over a year.

But there was a presence — someone else in the church! Every muscle braced; his hearing so sharp it was almost painful. Ken hadn't heard footsteps but now a man stood beside him.

He noticed first a long black coat and a pair of grimy feet in scuffed sandals. He glanced up. A tall, thin man with weary features and shoulder-length hair smiled down with an expression of patience and kindliness. Ken turned away and closed his eyes. Even here, he hadn't found the sanctuary he craved. Whoever he was, why couldn't he just go away?

'Are you alright?' queried a quiet voice.

I don't need this, thought Ken.

'Can I help? Would you like to talk?'

'Probably "no" to both,' muttered Ken. 'Just go away, just go away.' Had he spoken? *Just go away* kept hammering in his brain.

'May I sit with you?'

Ken slid along the dark, glossy wood; was he marking space between them? He should never have come to this place with its peculiar smells and even more peculiar practices. *I know nothing about these institutions*, he thought. *They're plain weird.*

Could this intruder edging into the pew have an answer to some of the endless questions spinning through his brain? He remained half-kneeling, clutching the pew in front.

He felt a light touch on one shoulder. 'Would it help to talk?'

Where to start or even whether to even *begin* telling his story? In the past, talking tended to make things worse. Ken squirmed, he hated being hassled — now there was no escape. Should he tell the man to butt out?

He'd been down this 'talking road' before; it only stirred emotions and bitter feelings, the last embarrassment he needed. There'd never been answers in all those months. No comfort, nothing that made sense even from professional psychologists, police counsellors, let alone family and friends.

He pulled out a handkerchief, blew his nose and sat back, half-turning away from the sandalled man. 'I don't make a habit of this ... haven't been to church since I was eleven. Shouldn't be here now — bothering. I came for ...' Why had he come?

The man beside him remained silent. In the stillness, Ken, despite himself, found the all too bleak story spilling out yet again. He told of his wife's disappearance — just over a year ago. At first the words came awkwardly, gathering momentum as the sadness and emotion challenged him. It was always the same once he started — an overwhelming sensation of loss, confusion and guilt. His shoulders shuddered as his voice blurred with tears of helplessness.

'What was her name?'

Her name? Ken held his breath. Her name? 'It was … it was … Freya.' For months he hadn't heard her name. Surely with the original publicity, *everyone* knew her name? Shaken that in wanting to block out the painful memories of a deeply loved wife, in a moment of nervous tension, her name had all but disappeared.

The man made no comment, but in his empathy Ken felt he had a connection with his own heartbreak.

He faltered, wiped his eyes and continued telling of that terrible day. How she'd gone to work as a PA, happily as far as Ken knew, and never came home. No one had an answer — not even her workmates. It seemed she'd never arrived in the office. Her colleagues were as mystified as he. Her bank account remained untouched — she was gone, vanished. The police found nothing of significance. Now, a year later, he felt they'd lost interest.

Apart from her make-up, her clothes and one of her rings, the green tourmaline, it was as if she'd never existed. 'The worst part,' said Ken, 'Is the not knowing … the silence. And I blame myself that if I had done something differently — I don't know what — we might have traced her? How can such a terrible thing happen in this day and age? How can I go on like this? There is now a dark hole beside me where once stood my darling Freya.'

As the words continued to flow, he spoke of his helplessness, his loneliness and feelings of rejection. People he'd thought friends slipped into doorways or turned corners to avoid him. He knew only too well what that meant. He'd been guilty of the same thoughtless reasoning. What could they possibly say to him that was helpful or a comfort?

As time went by he began to feel that the man was less of an intruder into his grief. 'I feel I should carry a lettered board around my neck. It says, "Avoid this man, he's an embarrassment". What I *have* done or what *should* I have done are endless questions with no answers.'

Ken lost all sense of time, hearing only the twittering of sparrows coming home to roost. By the time Freya's story had reached its end the birds were settled, the hum of the internal heating the only sound.

The sinking sun moved the stained glass splashes along the pew like sunflowers following the sun. Conscious only of a kindly human presence, Ken hadn't noticed the hand lift from his shoulder.

He raised his head, pushed against the pew in front and leaned back. How long had he been there by himself? About to stand, he felt again the press of a hand on his shoulder. The words were the same, 'Are you alright?' Ken opened his eyes.

A stocky man with a ruddy face stood beside him, shiny-pated but for a fringe of silver above his ears. He'd heard neither footsteps nor the opening or closing of the great door that could be inferred as either a barrier to entry or a shield against a cruel world.

The man wore a white surplice over a black cassock. The surplice so light it floated about the wearer, reminding Ken of the angels depicted in the deeply set window glass. Glancing beyond the man's shoulder, Ken saw the interior was now softly lit, but the church remained empty.

Ken replied, 'Thank you. I'm alright now, I talked to the other man.'

The churchman sat on the pew across the aisle, leaned forward, elbows on knees, hands clasped. 'What other man? There's no one else here.'

'The tall man with the long black coat. He was here, right beside me. I talked for a long time. He didn't say anything, he just listened.'

'Oh yes!' The priest hesitated. 'Yes, I think I know who you mean.'

'He had remarkable patience. It was what I needed. Just to talk it through — it was such a relief. Who is he?'

'He comes in here often.' The cleric smiled. 'I suppose I shouldn't tell you this, but he's a drifter, we let him sleep in the crypt. We know something of his story — he's a good man. Who did you think he was?'

From his seat Ken stared across at the priest. 'I have no idea!' A half-smile wrinkled around his eyes. He stood and shook the priest's hand. 'A friend, I would say. But I don't suppose it really matters.'

One who knows how to show and to accept kindness will be a **friend** better than any possession.

SOPHOCLES

SOS

John O'Neill

Fiachra O'Connell came north on the slow looping train from Inverness to the radio station at Wick in the autumn of 1947, when the Caithness moorland was already dying back into hibernation. He was immediately renamed Paddy by the lowland Scots who made up the normal complement of telegraph operators manning this indispensable link to the hundreds of boats fishing the frigid seas between Scotland and the Arctic. The only other 'furriner' was Taff, the elderly Welshman, who ruled the station despite his lowly official status by sheer force of McGoo-like bellicosity in a tiny frame. If Paddy ever hoped for support from a fellow 'expat' he was very quickly disillusioned.

Taff was a professional, come ashore after many years at sea in the radio rooms of great liners, tramp steamers and the boats which he now guarded, as part-time wireless officer, part-time boiler of fish oil from the great shoals of West Atlantic cod. Paddy was raw — straight out of telegraphy school and Bere Island in County Cork. His Morse was adequate if not yet second-nature. His knowledge of shipping was minimal. His accent was such that even in normal circumstances he and the Aberdeen boatmen understood each other with difficulty and, in moments of stress, his excited and accelerated delivery forced Taff to replace him on the radiotelephone. He was relegated, where possible, to the chores of Morse telegraphy, beating out weather forecasts and the accumulated messages for ships which had not made contact during the day — tedious work from which Paddy would often walk to his rooms with his right arm numb by his side. Paddy and Taff worked together grudgingly, avoided each other where possible and differed in every physical way and on every topic of conversation. Paddy was a physical shambles — 6 feet tall and not yet in control of his body. Taff was tiny but neat, quick and dapper in all he did and in the mustard-tweed plus-foured suit he wore on all occasions. They were a great trial, each to the other.

Until one night shift a few months after Paddy's arrival. They were on duty together. The others had gone home gratefully, through driving sleet, on the stroke of midnight. Paddy broadcast the backlog of messages from boat owners to captains, fish wives to husbands; all the everyday stuff of happy birthdays, sad and sometimes acrimonious family messages and the essentials of fishing news. At 0040 Taff went to the kitchenette to make tea while Paddy sat in listening watch on the telegraph calling and distress frequency, 500kc/s. Tea for Taff was a labour of love, an eclectic amalgam of teamaking ceremonies from around the world: boil water, add tea, stir one minute, add more water, more tea, allow to stand three minutes, decant and drink; amber, no sugar. Paddy could not enjoy his normal slapdash milk and two sugars on Taff's watch, so he slumped resignedly at the receiver, monitoring calls from ships as far as the Mediterranean, coming in clearly in the night. At 0045 silence descended on the channel, broken only by the massive blast 'QRT' (stop sending), on full power from North Foreland station to some idiot who continued to chatter his key well into the silence period. Paddy felt the silence deepen as his ears attuned: the only sound the hiss of static and random electrons in his receiver. The three-minute silence was almost up when he heard the call — SOS SOS SOS — strength one but readable. Taff was beside him with the tea ceremony as he unplugged his earphones and opened up the speakers.

'Oh God,' said Taff, 'that's Norman Jones on the *Island Queen*. I'd know his fist anywhere. Send SOS all stations, Paddy, keep the channel quiet while I phone coastguard — not that it'll make any difference, they're off Greenland.'

Paddy did what he was told, blasting out his QRT to those who started calling again after the silence period ended. Aided by many other stations around the North Atlantic, the message spread and an eerie silence was established. Taff came back. 'I'll take over, Paddy,' he said, and slipped into the control desk. Paddy picked up the nearest phones and stood over another receiver to listen in.

'QRA' (what is the name of your station?), sent Taff, unnecessarily but for the record. The answer confirmed Taff's identification as Norman and Taff established understanding of the crisis. The *Island Queen*, out of Aberdeen, was laden with cod after three weeks fishing in Greenland waters. They had hauled the nets for the last time and had turned for home. Off Iceland the storm had descended and then the icing started on the decks, masts, rigging; anywhere the spray could reach. They fought it with steam jets but it gained in weight until the boat wallowed in ever-increasing arcs and took water into the engine room, eventually killing all power and depriving them of the steam which had been their salvation. Norman had switched to battery power and sent his distress messages by the light of a hurricane lamp.

All this detail came out later as Taff recreated the scene from his personal experience. Only the basic needs were transmitted — location, strength of wind and wave, degrees of danger, state of batteries, etc. By now all ships and shore stations in the area were on alert and considering how they could help. The Icelandic fleet was a hundred miles away and desperately weathering the storm that had damaged the *Queen* and left her helpless. Two of them tried to fight their way into the northerly gale but were making only slow progress.

Taff kept up the contact, sending all the information available, encouraging where possible, while Paddy helped with the telephone, R/T, map references and latest weather.

Taff turned to Paddy. 'Their batteries are dying. I can barely hear him.'

Paddy checked on his receiver, 'I can hear him still,' and wrote down the message for Taff.

TAKING TO THE RAFT. GB OM TKS.

'He's locked the key down for anyone out there to beam in on.'

'I just can't hear it,' said Taff, angry and frustrated as he fiddled with the receiver. 'There's no one out there', he continued. 'Only God could save them now and the last fisherman he saved was Peter on that pond in Galilee.'

'And look at the thanks He got,' muttered Paddy, then stopped and, cupping his hands over his earphones, he listened with total intensity, his body still, compelling silence. 'It's stopped,' he said.

'Are you sure?' asked Taff. 'Did it fade out?'

'No,' said Paddy, 'it was weak but steady and then it stopped.'

'She's gone,' whispered Taff and grabbed the key, sending SOS and calling the *Queen*, over and over. Then he called the ships trying to steam north. Had they any contact, he demanded. They only confirmed what Paddy had heard but said the storm was easing and they would be on location by daybreak.

The hours passed with no relief. The *Queen* still made no response. Taff never stopped listening, calling, begging for a reply, urging on the rescuers. Then they found debris, ice-coated on a slick-laden ocean and, finally, the empty life raft. They had no hope and Taff was silent at last.

'Shouldn't we call off the distress?' asked Paddy, for the second time. Taff said nothing, then threw his earphones on the desk and walked away. Paddy went on air, announced the distress was lifted and heard first one, then another ship call, almost apologetically, with normal traffic.

They handed over to the incoming watch as grey light dawned. Taff said nothing. Paddy passed on the necessary information but dodged all questions and walked out with Taff into the gloom of the granity, early morning town. They did not speak even as they went their separate ways under the streetlamp by Taff's gate.

❈

When Taff arrived at the station that evening, Paddy was already in the kitchen making tea to start his shift. Taff talked sadly and seriously to the outgoing operators as Paddy watched through the glass door. Then he poured the tea carefully — black, no sugar — and brought it to Taff, who accepted it without comment and continued the discussion. A minute later Taff took a mouthful of tea, holding it momentarily before swallowing. He grimaced, his mouth contorted, and he turned on Paddy.

'Now I'm going to have to teach you how to make tea, you great Irish pillock.'

The room was quiet for a moment. Then the group dissolved into laughter: first the listeners, then Paddy and, finally, Taff himself. Normal life had been rekindled but changed intimately. So it was when Taff took early retirement a few weeks later, Paddy was the safe custodian of the secret reason for his departure.

The
wonderful
thing is that it's
so incredibly
easy to be kind.

INGRID NEWKIRK

AUNTY MAY

Shirley Vidovich

My Aunty May was born Hilda May Millicent Walsh. To us she was just Aunty May. She lived with her brother, Uncle Alec, in East Fremantle, Western Australia. Neither of them had been married, and we (my sisters and I) wanted to know why not. There was talk that Aunty May had been turned down by a married man whom she had chased and Uncle Alec had a stiff leg from his childhood, so these were possible reasons. Not very good ones.

When we were little children they used to invite us over at New Year and we would eat well and play games with Aunty May. We would overeat with such delicacies as plums, peaches, apricots and assorted nuts. Aunty May would play children's games with us. They usually ended up creepy games, but we didn't mind, as we enjoyed them. Especially the one where the clock strikes midnight and all of us count down the hours. Then the zombies would come out. Everyone, including the adults, would join in a game of hide and seek and that was great fun. We would hide in the sleepout, then slide back the windows and race to home base without the seeker spotting us. Home base was just 100 metres away.

At Christmas time Aunty and Uncle would celebrate at our house. Sometimes, we would have as many as twenty people attending, but Aunty and Uncle remained our favourites. Now and again they would get the presents mixed up and behind the scenes a whole lot of swapping and exchanging would go on. As they got older, the shopping for presents became a chore, so they used to buy an extraordinary amount of chocolate and give each of us huge blocks in a parcel. Sometimes as many as five blocks of chocolate. That was alright with us. They were generous with their nieces.

Aunty May belonged to the Salvation Army and was an Envoy, the lowest rung in the chain of positions. She loved her work and always tried to make people happy. Her area for her work was the Fremantle area. She would always ride a bicycle. This bicycle would always be laden down with *War Cry*, the Salvation Army paper, collection boxes and other articles required for her job. Often people would ridicule her, as she was a sight to behold. An elderly lady riding a bike, laden down with all sorts of equipment, and one marvels that she didn't fall off the bicycle. Aunty May was most likely described as eccentric. She would collect inside the hotels and outside public events such as football matches and racing. I can remember hoping she wouldn't be there if I were with friends. She would also attend my school as the religious instructor. At that age I found it embarrassing, but I soon learnt to live with these feelings and never felt ashamed that she was my aunty again. Blood is thicker than water. My closest sisters and I would be invited to play at an annual concert at the Salvation Army. We would play a trio, the three of us playing on the same piano at the one time. We were popular, as most people hadn't heard of a trio before. Duets, yes. We enjoyed the applause when we had completed the item.

My father, her brother, was very protective of my aunty. If he was drinking in a hotel and saw Aunty May come in, he would say to the people he was drinking with to put their glasses down. I don't know what this would have achieved; if you are in a hotel you would drink. The same would apply if he was at home with Uncle Alec. If May came into a room, he would indicate to Alec to put his glass down and hide it. She still knew what went on, but Dad didn't want her to know.

'Here's May,' he would say and promptly hide his glass.

As May grew older, she still rode her bicycle. One day it went missing and it was a bad day for her, as she couldn't do her work. Some men who drank at the bars in the Fremantle area all clubbed in to buy her a new bicycle, as they had heard about the loss of her bike. She was so pleased and thankful. She was touched that they would do that for her. Their generosity was held close to her heart and she firmly believed that people are good. Aunty May was an identity in the Fremantle area. Everybody knew her and the work she did.

One day at breakfast, Dad was flicking through the papers and he stopped and said, 'Crikey, May's been awarded the Order of Australia.'

We rushed over to the paper and there, in black and white, she had been given an Order of Australia for work among the needy and helping people to find their way. My mother accompanied Aunty May to Government House to receive her award from Sir

John Kerr and it was an exciting day for our family. Imagine the excitement in getting ready to receive the medal. She was very proud. It was in a velvet lined box and the various parts of it were in sunken grooves among the velvet. I think my eldest sister retained the medal, but she has recently died, so I really don't know where it is.

Unfortunately, it was all downhill from there. Small things gave the indication that Aunty was suffering from dementia. Thinking back, we realized this may have started years earlier, as she often came to our place. Dad said she may have been lost in the streets, so called in to our place. The Christmas present mix-ups may have been the onset of dementia. Frequently she was getting lost when out on her bike and too many things were burning on the stove. Now she had attained the age of 84. She was taken in to hospital care, but she had a habit of running away, so had to be restrained. Can you imagine how we felt when we visited her and saw the restraints keeping her in the chair? It seems almost draconian now. However, despite her health worries, she had a fulfilling life and was rewarded with her medal. So, if you are good to other people you do get a reward.

How many people get this medal?

Not many.

Never look down on anybody unless you're **helping** them up.

JESSE JACKSON

ROUGH SLEEPER

Margaret Callow

They are everywhere, not in just one town or city, but simply wherever there is a doorway, a park bench, an underpass or a shop front. Hopefully where some light might protect them and warmth succour their cold bones. Mostly men, it seems. Commonplace like litter blown into a kerb and needing no more than the space a body would require to curl up. To sleep, mostly. The daylight hours are easier to fill. Watching people pass. Hoping for a coin tossed their way. Most must rely on such things.

Freshly obtained benefits are for more essentials requisites. Tobacco, a 'tinnie' or two, or three, maybe a bottle of something stronger and the pacifier of all bad dreams and ugly memories, the elixir of the poppy fields. Little left for a proper meal.

Put a mirror to the eyes of the passer-by and what might you notice? Pity, sympathy, scorn, concern even or perhaps the blank look of one who sees but is blind. Although usually late for work, Kit's thoughtful eyes never avoided the recumbent forms, but she would give them no more than a passing glance. Until this morning. This morning was different.

The doorway to start with. It was one she had never seen occupied before, despite her route never varying. A new member of the rough sleepers' group, perhaps? Perhaps not — something seemed different. The man's position, to start with. No hump under a collection of old rugs and cardboard, no sorrowful features above a soiled blanket gathered up to a thin neck. Not even in a comfortable position, if comfort could be had from hard paving slabs or a skinny, threadbare cushion.

Kit's footsteps slowed. The more she pondered, the more she was sure the man might have fallen. Or maybe been pushed. His head, which lolled on his chest, revealed dark hair, a lot of it, no obvious strands of grey and he certainly looked in an awkward shape. A quick glance at her watch told her she should be almost at the office by now. To stay or go — how often are we forced into that situation?

Another look at the recumbent figure and her compassion won the day. The man's smart tweed jacket, expensive looking cord pants and a tie didn't speak of poverty, far from it. Nor did a folded newspaper not far from his right hand. Kit approached him and leaned down, watched by the bemused eyes of passing commuters. Her sniff was genteel, discreet, an imperceptible movement of her nose. She couldn't detect alcohol, the air as fresh as any shop doorway might be, allowing for diesel and other exhaust fumes, and she felt slightly guilty. Not an intoxicated vagrant, then.

At the same time, the man stirred and lifted his head. His pallor and the sweat on his brow alarmed her. Her mind raced. Had he been attacked? Injured? Was he ill? The adverts about detecting strokes had not been lost on her, but hard to tell just the same.

'Are you alright?' she asked.

His eyes took a moment to focus. One hand clutched at empty space. He looked bewildered. Kit crouched down closer and said, 'Sorry, silly question. Can I help at all?'

It seemed an age before he replied, then he looked at her directly and muttered, 'Sweet.'

She didn't know whether to laugh or feel offended. In the end, humour won and she grinned.

'That's very kind of you, but I'm not sure …'

He shook his head. This time his hand directed itself onto her wrist. Firm fingers painfully tight on her flesh. The words, slightly slurred, came out in a rush, 'No, a sweet, do you have a sweet, a piece of chocolate, any biscuits? I need sugar, didn't feel well, must have fallen.'

It made sense now — he must be a diabetic. Never had Kit wished her bag tidier. She scrabbled through its contents. How many pens did she carry? And lipsticks, at least three swaddled in tissues. Hand wipes too, her purse, spare glasses, more tissues, a button, blue tattered diary two years out of date. Her fingers went faster searching. A safety pin, several plasters too tatty for use and then at last a rustling noise.

A butterscotch sweet living alone in the dark recesses of her handbag's lining. Clearly an outcast from the rest of the bag dwellers. When she finally managed to free it, it stuck to her fingers. 'Sorry, I only have one,' she said, doubtful she would ever prise it from its cellophane wrapper.

'That'll help,' he mumbled. 'It's my fault, didn't bother with much breakfast. Usually carry a bit of glucose or at least a couple of biscuits. Today, nothing. You'd think I'd know by now.' He managed a rueful smile.

She watched the colour return to his cheeks. 'It's very good of you, to stop, that is,' he said. 'I felt it coming on, you always do, but everyone is in such a hurry and then there are the ones who just look the other way. Thank you for helping.'

'It was just a sweet,' she replied, wondering why the world had changed so much.

Are people so immersed in their own business they have no time for others? Maybe they are frightened by events like terrorism and therefore unwilling to stop in an unknown situation? Or is that too extreme? Are they just too selfish to think of others before themselves? Too busy looking after number one to find time to help a fellow being?

What is clear is human kindness should have no boundaries. It is within us all to hold out a hand to someone in need and woeful is the day we are so busy helping ourselves to spare a moment to help another.

When we give cheerfully and accept gratefully, everyone is blessed.

MAYA ANGELOU

THE PARTY

Susie Anderson

My son was horrified when I offered to mend his jeans, the ones with the holes in the knees. He said he had paid a lot of money for them in a shop down the road. I saw that shop; it had nothing in the window except a fake plastic hand dripping with blood. This son told me he no longer needs a mother. He said he would be happy to have me as a friend but not a mother. 'Those days are gone,' he said firmly.

My son is having a birthday party. No, I think I need to rephrase that. I am having a birthday party.

Let's go back to the beginning.

We are sitting at the kitchen table eating sausage rolls and tomato sauce. I hate sausage rolls. After you swallow them they sit inside you for ages, hardly moving. But he likes them. He says, 'It's my birthday next week.' Well I would remember that, wouldn't I, as I was there when he was born. He says he would like to have a party with a few of his friends. I think this is a very nice idea. I also like celebrating birthdays, so I say, 'That would be fun.' There is an odd pause while he dips the sausage roll in the tomato sauce. As I am not eating anything, I speak.

'Where were you thinking of having this party?'

There is another pause, even longer than the one before, as he wipes his red-stained fingers on the white linen serviette. Now this son is quite bright. He did well in his first-year university exams, so I wonder, *What is wrong here?* I repeat, 'Where would you like to have this birthday party? Maybe that pizza place you like near the beach? Or the sushi café near your flat?'

His shoulders droop, his mouth sags. There is a slight frown drawing his eyebrows into a straight line.

'The trouble is,' he says, with a slight tremble in the voice, 'I am not too financial at the moment.' I viciously think of the shop with the bloody hand and wonder why he bought the jeans with holes that cost more than my gas bill. He studies the sausage roll.

'You know what I thought last night riding home on my bike?'

He looks happier now. I wonder if he met that pretty girl he likes on his bike ride home. He continues.

'I was thinking how good it would be to have the party outside, like a barbecue.' I look quizzically at him.

'But you don't have an outside. You have a fire escape.'

I do have a mean streak. He looks mournfully out of the window.

'That's true and it's a very small fire escape. Just a landing really.'

I know how small it is. When he moved there I helped carry suitcases and clothes and books, a heater and a CD player up those stairs onto that landing in the rain.

His gaze is riveted outside the window. He looks puzzled.

'What is the name of that tree out there?'

I am a little startled, as he has never shown any interest in my garden or my tree. Nothing is diverting him now from that tree. He tilts his head in a charming way. 'It's so cool, the way the branches hang down over the table and chairs out there in your courtyard.'

I can hardly believe my ears when I hear myself say, 'Would you like to have the birthday party out there? At my place?'

His face is a picture of surprise and delight. He really should take up acting. He gets up quite quickly and heads down the hall. As he makes his way towards the front door, his voice wafts back to me.

'Keep it simple won't you? Don't fuss, just a few snags, some steaks, a salad or two. I'll ask a few mates, say around ten or so. Bye. See ya. Lovely idea.'

Peace begins with a smile.

MOTHER TERESA

HUMAN KINDNESS IN OCCUPIED GERMANY

John Fletcher

When the war ended in Europe in May 1945, my father was a technical civil servant based in London. He was employed by the Aeronautical Inspection Directorate, part of the Ministry of Supply. He and his family — which consisted of my mother, my younger brother and me — lived in various places around the capital, depending on where, at the time, the threat of German air attack was felt to be less serious. On a couple of occasions, at the height of the bombing, we even moved to Yeovil, Somerset, my father's birthplace.

In 1945 he was seconded to the Allied Control Commission, Germany. His duties did not involve aircraft inspection. He worked in demolition (after what training, if any, I have no idea). He took me once to watch him blow up a bunker. Whenever I see on television a block of flats collapsing or a factory chimney slowly disintegrating, I wonder how my father would have set about calculating the explosive charge needed to bring the whole thing down with minimal collateral damage.

He went to Germany ahead of his family. We followed in 1946. We had to receive a series of inoculations because it was feared infectious diseases would break out in a country where most of the infrastructure had been destroyed or badly damaged. We spent a few days in bed afterwards, feeling very ill. But we soon recovered. We then embarked on a troopship at Tilbury for what, to a child, seemed like a long sea crossing. The food on board was rich — we had been used to rationing — and we were sick, not so much from the rolling motion of the vessel, but from overeating.

My father, who up till then had lived in military quarters, had requisitioned a house for us on Graf-Adolf-Strasse in Altena, a small town in the western part of the Sauerland. It was normal for Allied personnel to find a house they liked the look of and then tell the owners to move out within days. The one he chose was a rather grand villa standing in its own grounds. It was situated on a steep hill on the outskirts of town. My father had bought one of the first Volkswagens to roll off the production line after the war, and the reassuring sound of the car changing gear as he drove up the hill home will remain with me forever.

There were so many good things about our life in Germany, but all was not sweetness and light. The bad things — such as the jagged skyline of bombed Bielefeld, where my father was posted next — will remain burnt on to my retinas for as long as I live. But fortunately, a child cannot understand the concept of carpet bombing. Bomb sites even became my playground. I ran about freely with young German boys who were as ignorant as I was about the reason for the destruction of the buildings we frolicked in. While playing with them I became, without realizing it, fluent in German. I have lost my fluency since, but I have kept my good accent: Germans assume that I am a native speaker until I run out of words, and even today I surprise myself by how much passive knowledge I have retained. Whenever I watch a German documentary on television I find that, with some assistance from subtitles, I can understand all of it.

Playing with German boys once saved my younger brother's life. We were skating on a local lake when the ice gave way and he fell in. Fortunately he was wearing a knitted balaclava helmet, and a couple of German boys were able to grab hold of this and haul him out of the freezing water. It was a great act of kindness on the part of young people who had scant reason to come to the assistance of the occupiers of their country.

British forces had at first been forbidden to 'fraternize' with the 'natives' — it really *was* a quasi-colonial situation — but that absurdity was soon relaxed, and my family then fraternized enthusiastically. My father would drive us high up into the heart of the Sauerland to a farm that was completely untouched by war and even by the modern world. The ploughing was done by docile carthorses on which I was allowed to ride. We supplemented our NAAFI rations with fresh meat and vegetables from the farm. In return we supplied them with soap, cigarettes and the other standard items of barter used at the time. But with us it was not really barter. It was more like an exchange of gifts, because we became close friends with the farmer's family. My mother picked up German quite quickly, so it did not matter that my father's German remained limited to phrases like '*aber schnell*' and '*viel Arbeit*'. So we were able to communicate with the farmer and his family, whose kindness I will never forget. On leaving Germany, we had to leave behind our much-loved Scottish terrier, Troll. They gladly took him in. I love to think of Troll living out his days on that farm in the Sauerland; I am sure he repaid their goodness of heart by speedily becoming a first-rate rat-catcher.

The ugly side of the situation in occupied Germany was, however, never far distant. Even as a child I was dimly aware of tensions between the western allies and the Soviet forces occupying Eastern Germany, tensions which would, quite soon, lead to the Berlin blockade and the Allied airlift of 1948. As we were leaving the farm one day the grandmother came up to our Volkswagen. She scrabbled on the windows and kept whimpering *'die Russen, die Russen'*. My father gently assured her that the Russians were a long way off and not about to overrun her farm. She was consoled by that act of kindness.

Although a civilian, my father wore British battledress (I still have the photo), and it was only recently that I discovered why. Knowing how things had developed in occupied countries between 1940 and 1945, the Allies feared that a partisan movement would arise in Germany. There were certainly plenty of weapons still lying around. When my brother and I played in the hills above our villa in Altena we would come across piles of abandoned ordnance which had not been disposed of. Had a *maquis* developed, they would no doubt have been able to use some of it. Of course, it never came to that. But as in countries occupied by the Wehrmacht, any partisan attack on a soldier in uniform would have been punishable by summary execution. So Dad, though a civilian, wore battledress.

I not only learnt to ride a horse in Germany, I learnt to ski as well. Alas, I soon forgot how, and now can no longer manage either. While we lived in Altena, my brother and I would roam the hills above our villa. One day we saw, by the side of the path, a handmade wooden cross. We assumed it marked a German soldier's grave. After that, we called the path 'soldier-cross path' and avoided that part of the woods. But we got into serious trouble once when we started playing with matches and set the undergrowth alight. We ran home in panic, and watched the smoke rising on the hill. The resulting forest fire apparently caused a lot of damage, and we were very severely told off by my father. Whether he had to pay for the damage, however, I doubt. He was, after all, a member of an occupying army and probably got away with a mild reprimand.

In Germany, Christmas is special. Even in the dark days of military occupation and of painfully slow reconstruction, Christmas was celebrated by occupier and occupied alike. And instead of weapons, German factories were now starting to make toys again. One Christmas I was given a train set, and it took my father most of Christmas Day to set it up. I was of course impatient to play with it, but until he'd finished I had to wait. I was reminded of that when my son-in-law spent 25 December 2014 setting up a train set for his little boy. Another time I got a clockwork-powered Dux Kino Modell 40, through which I threaded strips of film before projecting the moving images on to a white wall.

A new chapter in my life opened when my father was posted back to the United Kingdom, bringing to a close three extraordinary years. Those years — 1946 to 1949 — were among the happiest of my life. I have of course known happiness since, but there is no happiness like the happiness of childhood. In retrospect it is unclouded by the shadows that loom over us in later life; it was as if the sun shone every day and human kindness was universal.

The fragrance
always stays in
the hand that
gives the rose.

HADA BEJAR

THAT NOONTIME

Judy Light Ayyildiz

Embarrassed, I sneaked past the grade school cafeteria and out onto the playground. Couldn't even feel sorry for myself. My fault. Baloney sandwich on light bread with mustard and lettuce. In a brown paper poke on the kitchen table. Not even a nickel for a Hershey Bar.

Out the door and away from the other second grade kids eating, I passed by Roosevelt's WPA-built rock wall that held the grounds, bopping my hand along the top of the rough stones as if I had somewhere to go.

In an hour, I could hang outside until the bell rang; and then I'd go to my classroom. I'd ask the teacher if I could please go to the bathroom. By the time I got back, they would be doing math and no one would ask me why I wasn't at lunch.

I half-hoped something edible would fall out of the sky. I'd have some water when I went inside. There'd be a snack when we stopped off at Mrs Murphy's, the farmwife who sometimes kept us when Momma worked. Up a dirt road off Piedmont Road, Mrs Murphy's farm had pigs.

At first, there came the brushing sound. I glanced over to a red brick sidewalk that looked like dominoes. It led to a row of wooden steps up to a porch with white wooden railings. A big-size grandma stopped sweeping. The September light fell across her white hair and onto her shoulders. She smiled at me in the way my granny did. Her pretty frame house was only half a block from school, but I'd never before paid it any mind.

She looked up, pulling the broom handle to the breast of her blue and white apron. Her hair was kneaded back into a biscuit. A couple of hairs straggled down the side of her face. I knew from Granny that her deep-pocket apron and cozy body was like sinking into a well-worn smushy chair. The sparkles in her eyes stopped me short. Her brick path joined my sidewalk.

'To where be *you* bound on such a fine fall noontime?' she asked in a Good Fairy voice.

'Anywhere.'

I can't say how, but she seemed to have a special knowing about her, like one of those angels in disguise. The granny read my face from brow to chin. She leaned against her big broom with one hand and brought the other to her hip, and eyed me top to bottom. She asked me my name, and I told her, 'Judy.'

'Well, young lady, I'm Mrs Fairchild, and I dare say you've already had a big lunch.'

I focused down, onto the creases across the tops of her laced-up black shoes that stuck out from under an ankle-length blue skirt, and mumbled. 'I decided I didn't want lunch today.'

She brought the broom to the front of her and held it with both hands. I swear that I half-expected her to zoom off on it. Fairy Godmothers could do that. She laughed while she spoke.

'And don't that beat all! Here I was hoping to find myself someone willing to share my pot of fresh homemade chicken vegetable soup.'

I wavered, a little unsteady. 'What?' I asked in the tiniest voice.

She shook her head. 'I'd sure be obliged if you'd do me the favour of changing your mind and joining me at my kitchen table.'

My mouth dropped open. I could hardly contain myself. Nor could I believe my luck. As it turned out, I was given the chance to do an old lady a kindness — by having lunch.

'There just might be dessert,' she added, batting her lids into the happy lines that decorated the sides of her eyes.

Taking a quick look around me to make sure that no one had followed me — and to be certain that I was still on this street that ran by the school and not on some page of a book, I took in a happy breath.

Turning back, I said, 'Sure,' shrugging as if it didn't matter to me one way or the other.

She held out her hand and I gave mine. We bounced across dominoes on up to steps and a porch with two rockers and some pots of orangey chrysanthemums blooming like crazy.

Posting the broom against the wall beside the door, she opened the screen and held it for me while I passed through into the shaded light of her hallway. She was talking all the time about how welcome I should make myself as she followed me in and brushed around and bade me come on down the hall to the kitchen. The room spread out sunny with bluebells on a strip of wallpaper that went all around the edge of the ceiling, matching the bluebells and daisies in the oilcloth on the round table that sat between the window and back door.

'Just pull you up a chair,' she said over her shoulder. She had gone to the stove. The tall silver pot steamed up curly hints of tomatoes and chicken and green peppers and carrots and who could say what else, but I hoped noodles.

Into wide and heavy blue bowls with plates under them, she ladled soup; with me, all the time, reminding myself that I'd have to eat like a lady, although I knew I could just gobble up the whole bowlful like a yellow dog. And then, I was bug-eyeing the flat noodles.

She doled out slices of cheese with crackers. Soda crackers, my favourites. I knew then and there that this experience was something far too special to be real. Maybe I was still sitting by the wall in the playground and had fallen asleep.

Who cared!

She poured me a glass of milk and sat down and we ate and talked.

'So, young lady,' she said, looking straight into my eyes. 'You can call me Mrs Fairchild. And since you already told me your first name, I will call you Judy Garland!'

'Judy Garland!' I said. 'Our favourite!' Mrs Fairchild was nodding her head as if she completely got it.

'Momma was gonna name me after my aunt, who couldn't have any children. Aunt Mag was a midwife who helped Grannie deliver me; but Daddy was fond of Miss Garland.'

'Well, that's just who you'll be in my book.' I liked that idea. Judy Garland was a singer and very famous. She had big eyes.

'Were you a school teacher?'

'When I was twice your age, I went off to boarding school and started my way to be a teacher, Miss Garland.'

A drawing, I could make her a drawing of Twelve Pole Creek, and bring it to her. She'd like that.

The hour held us as if it and we were scooped out from the inside of the day.

All at once we were done, and there she was sending me back through the screen door with a second chocolate cookie.

Back in class, I told a handful of kids that Mrs Fairchild invited me to a fancy lunch just so she wouldn't have to eat alone. I didn't hesitate to add that who knows how often I might be invited again. Maybe I even embellished on it a little. Colouring up a tale was not lying, after all.

One of the town kids with a canvas flowered book bag rolled her eyes at my story. She stepped through the circle and stared into my face. 'Mrs Fairchild,' she said, as if I was lying, 'has been laid up in bed, waiting for her daughter in Pittsburgh to come and haul her up there so she can get an operation!'

'That's a ball-faced story you just made up!' I yelled. 'She said I look like Judy Garland!'

'Like fire, it is! My mom knows her and her whole family, and you're nothing but a country bumpkin who would never be invited to Mrs Fairchild's, especially the way you told it — and you don't look like nobody!' I was going to start crying so I spun around and went to the bathroom instead. I'd let them see me take my drawing over to Mrs Fairchild. They would listen while she called me Judy Garland.

I never saw Mrs Fairchild again. Walked past her house at least twice a week, but she was never outside. The house was as dark as if nobody lived there. I couldn't have just walked up to her porch and knocked. It would have looked like I was asking for something. I could have written her a thank you note and stuck it to the door but I had not told my parents about the lunch. It was easier to listen to how careless I had been in going off and leaving my lunch than it was to try to explain.

I had not been fed and taken in by a stranger. She was a Fairy Godmother.

Genuine kindness is no ordinary act, but a gift of rare beauty.

SYLVIA ROSSETTI

THE UNEXPECTED NATURE OF HUMAN KINDNESS

Dr Jacqueline Jaffrey

Whenever I read about the latest world tragedy, whether it be the latest terrorist attack in the Middle East, the hardships experienced in many third world countries, or the tragic plight of so many refugees languishing in camps that exist in appalling conditions, I remind myself that it is often the small acts of human kindness that sustain my optimism in humankind.

A good example of this was found during the fifteen months my family and I spent in Germany in 1979 and 1980. We were fortunate enough to spend a sabbatical leave in Saarbrücken in south-western Germany. When we told our friends in Australia that we planned to spend over a year there, mostly the responses we received were ones of pity as various stereotyped perceptions of Germans were thrown at us — 'They are so cold, unfriendly, arrogant, rigid.' These were the frequent pictures presented. Nothing could be further from the truth.

When our family arrived in Saarbrücken, we discovered that finding rented, furnished accommodation was almost unheard of, and we wondered if we would ever be able to find something suitable for a couple with two young children. One of the scientists with whom my husband would be working bent backwards to 'suss' out possibilities for us. Nothing was too much trouble. Eventually he found us a furnished house in a small village called St Ingbert, just outside Saarbrücken, that had been inherited by a middle-aged couple from the village. We signed the lease, and from the time we moved there, we encountered so many acts of human kindness.

One of our first challenges was organizing the billing for our electricity supply. The system there was based on estimating your likely usage. A man from the electricity board turned up the day after we moved there in order to interview us about our likely needs. He spoke no English, and I had only a small smattering of German. That did not deter this delightful, jovial man. He spent two hours with me, whereby through a series of mutual drawings, we managed to communicate and come up with a reasonably accurate estimate. His patience was to be commended, as drawing was never one of my strengths. As he prepared to leave, he pulled out of his pocket some chocolate eggs for the children. His kindness was typical of many Germans we met.

I guess many might classify the Martins (our landlord and his wife) as uneducated peasant class, but their generosity toward us is something I will cherish forever. They often popped in to see us — not to spy on us or intrude, but just to check that all was well. Each visit brought little treats for the children and often fresh produce from their garden. Their honesty and warmth gradually made them into our surrogate parents. This was brought home to us when it was time to leave. We were driving to the north of Germany in order to catch a ferry to England, where we had planned to spend the final six months of our extended sabbatical. We stopped at a guesthouse for the night in a small town near where we would be catching our ferry. We had just settled into our room, when my husband discovered that his wallet was missing. We had had a farewell meal at our landlord's house just before we left St Ingbert, so as my husband mentally retraced his steps he realized it had probably fallen out of his pocket at Herr Martin's place. In dismay, he rang the Martins. Herr Martin answered the phone and the relief in his voice was unmistakable. It turned out that when he discovered the wallet, he tried to work out some way of contacting us. Remember, these were before the days of mobile phones. Consequently, he contacted the police and the local radio stations to announce that the wallet was safely with them. How many people would go to so much trouble? As the guesthouse where we were staying was nearly six hours' drive from St Ingbert, Herr Martin insisted on driving north and meeting my husband halfway so that we would not miss our ferry the following morning.

Another fond memory I have of the kindness of the local villagers was when the first decent snow fall came. Of course, as temporary residents we did not have sleds or toboggans, but we decided to walk over to the local hill, so that at least our children could watch the other children engage in snow play. Within minutes of arriving there, a German family approached us and offered their toboggan for our children to use. We had never met this couple before. Our children were thrilled and had a wonderful afternoon in the snow.

Perhaps one of the most moving acts of kindness we experienced took place about a month after we had moved to St Ingbert. Our two children, aged six and eight, were enrolled in the local primary school (*grundschüle*) after Christmas. I discovered the hard way that the system was very different to that in Australia. The school day ran from 8 a.m. to 11.30 a.m. each morning, a very short school day by our standards. I had been lucky enough to obtain a part-time teaching job at the university, so I organized a babysitter to come to our home each day at about the time the children were due to arrive home. I thought I had all contingencies covered. How wrong I was! I arrived home about 2.30 in the afternoon to find a note on the door, informing me that our daughter was at our neighbour's house across the road. This puzzled me, as I barely knew this neighbour. With apprehension, I ran across the road to her house. She greeted me warmly and reassured me that all was well. It turned out that in this region, if a teacher falls ill and cannot teach that day, the children from that class are sent home, rather than the system I knew — a casual teacher brought in to cover the class. Our daughter arrived home on that very cold wintery morning and sat on the step, upset and unsure what to do. Fortunately, our neighbour spotted her and immediately rescued her. She had made such a fuss over our little one that she was reluctant to come home. She was having such a good time. This neighbour not only plied me with coffee and cakes as I calmed down, but also insisted that she would happily mind our daughter should this happen again. We became good friends from that day on.

Throughout our time in Germany, we did not experience those stereotypical images painted by our friends, but only warmth and generosity. Rarely a week went by when we did not experience some spontaneous act of kindness.

It was with great sadness that we boarded that ferry to leave Germany. Even now, nearly 40 years later, those wonderful memories sustain my faith in human nature. I am now a grandparent and accept that my grandsons are living in a far more complicated world than that time. However, it is those small acts of kindness that remind me that human goodness will always exist.

No act of kindness, no matter how small, is ever wasted.

AESOP

A GOOD JUDGE OF CHARACTER

Kate Amesbury

Jesus lived at the bottom of the grubby, tiled stairwell in our block of flats, which stood like an enormous tombstone at the end of the stinging, sand-blasted street. Behind us towered brooding volcanic mountains, and in front, shimmering in the heat, Slave Island and the beach, where skeletons of old *dhows* lay rotting in the mud like stranded whales.

I'd never known anyone called Jesus before, apart from Jesus in the Bible, and my mother was so traumatized by his name, and appearance, that she said it amounted to nothing short of blasphemy. She refused to acknowledge him, which was strange, because she wasn't of the Christian faith.

My mother had always been a good judge of character, so I couldn't fathom what it was about Jesus that she found to be so offending. The other residents of the flats had assured her that Jesus was trustworthy, helpful and always eager to wash cars or run errands.

Jesus didn't seem to own much. He dressed simply, wearing just a striped cotton sarong and a white *koofiya*, to shield his head from the scorching sunshine. His most precious possession was his *djambia*, the traditional weapon worn by Yemeni men to show their wealth and status in society. It was a dagger with a wickedly curved blade, the handle being carved from rhinoceros horn, in the belief that the owner would become as strong as the rhino.

Jesus certainly did look tough, and the weathered texture of his skin reminded me of my grandmother's dining table: burnished ebony, the dark veneer bashed and scratched with over 400 years of history. I didn't know how old Jesus was, but he seemed to be engraved with the same magnitude of time. From the wrinkles on his beaming face, to the savage keloid scar that travelled down from his left collarbone to just above his belly button, it was obvious he had more tales to tell than history. Heavy silver rings of Arabian design glittered on his left hand, but on his right, no fingers to adorn … sheared off by a shark when he'd gone fishing, so he said, but my mother said it was more likely they'd been chopped off as a punishment for theft.

Jesus spent many of his afternoons intoxicated. *Khat*, the green leaves of paradise, rendered him comatose for hours. When he finally emerged, with his cheeks still packed with masticated leaves, he'd go for a pee behind the parked cars and then briskly wash himself down at the rusted tap in the wall. Removing the sticky wads of *khat* from his mouth, he'd make a loud rasping noise in his throat, sounding like he was dragging up the entire contents of his stomach, then he'd retch, emitting a large gobbet of yellow phlegm.

Returning to the stairwell, he'd take out his prayer mat, unroll it and kneel down to give praise to God. When he had finished his devotion, he'd carefully roll the mat up again, then squat down under the stairwell to brew himself some watery coffee on his small gas camping stove. With a frowning expression, he'd listen to the Arabic news on his battered transistor radio, which was hung up on the wall beside his cracked shaving mirror.

I always remember how he ate his chapatti bread, dipping it into his hot coffee, then munching slowly, open-mouthed, flashing the gold fillings in his *khat*-stained teeth.

'Here, Chicco, you hungry?' he'd ask, offering me a large portion of his meagre chapatti. I gave him a peanut butter sandwich, left over from my school lunchbox.

For most of us children, Yemen, and the city of Aden, was our first experience of a foreign country, and we felt like we'd stepped off the plane straight into a biblical landscape that had the fairytale elements of Narnia, except we had sand instead of snow, and Jesus was our beloved Mr Tumnus. Some children were used to changing countries every few years, having recently arrived from air force bases in Beirut, Cyprus or Singapore, and they proved to be a curious mixture of ill-mannered brats and savages who had many bizarre tales to tell of foreign lands.

On some days, Beverly, Andrew, myself and our group of six to ten year olds, would pack into Jesus's cramped stairwell. Sitting like nomads, we'd lean in, listening keenly to each other's amazing stories. Jesus always recited the best adventures, especially the ones about crossing Rub al Khali, the Empty Quarter, and being bitten by scorpions hiding in the sands. Or tales about sailing on a *dhow* to Mombasa and fighting pirates, which was how he received the deep wound across his torso.

There were some days when Jesus had no time for us — usually at Ramadan, when he grew short-tempered with lack of food. So we looked elsewhere for amusement. We played on the stairs, or in each other's flats, but exasperated parents kept telling us to play somewhere else. So we did … up on the roof, where the *dhobi wallah* hung out the washing. With the lines of laundry billowing in the warm air, the roof became our galleon in full sail, and we were pirates. It was Andrew who started the game with the water-filled balloons, and then Beverly, always the devil, decided to climb over the low perimeter wall and out onto the parapet. She crawled on her hands and knees to the edge and peeped over.

'Get a look at this!' she yelled. 'Come on, or are you chicken?'

Eleven stories up we lay on the parapet, staring down into the busy street far below. Then Andrew dropped his water balloon. It exploded on the pavement near two men waiting at a bus stop. They looked up, and one of them strode purposely towards the flats.

'He's coming to get us!' shrieked Beverly.

Everyone quickly shuffled back from the edge and scrambled over the wall to safety.

Left on my own, I shook with fear and couldn't move. I screwed up my eyes and wailed. Then, just as I thought I was going to plunge earthwards like the water-filled balloon, I was hauled backwards.

Jesus was leaning over the wall, his good hand holding my ankle, the other, fingerless, reaching out towards me. I grasped it, and he pulled me to safety.

'You play very dangerous game!' he scolded. 'I tell your fathers what you do. You very bad chiccos.'

Later that day, Jesus came knocking at our door. I hid in the kitchen, thinking he was going to tell on us. My mother wasn't happy to see him.

'Memsahib,' said Jesus, looking around furtively. 'Tonight, Chicco's not play out. Stay safe inside. Please ... you tell all memsahibs.' Then he darted downstairs before my mother had a chance to question him.

'That man knows more than he's saying,' she said to my father, when he came home from work. 'Someone should report him!'

When evening came all the residents barricaded themselves inside, not knowing what to expect. By half past eight nothing had happened, and my younger sister and I were sent to bed. Then our world shook. The explosion was so loud that my ears popped and the glass in our window shattered, the force throwing the bedroom curtains upwards, where they became momentarily horizontal.

My parents rushed into our bedroom, but my eldest sister arrived first, running out from the bathroom in just her bra and knickers. She had curlers in her hair, and the pins pricked our cheeks as she hugged us both tightly. I knew she was screaming, but I couldn't hear anything as my ears were whistling.

A terrorist bazooka had hit the flat next door. No one was killed that night, but sadly for us children, Jesus vanished from our lives. At first, we thought my mother had reported him and he'd been arrested, but she said she hadn't, and no one else knew anything. Whoever Jesus was, we children loved him. He had become a trusted friend — a playmate, a guardian angel — and the loss was devastating when we saw the empty stairwell every morning when we went downstairs to the school bus.

The terrorist threat was now tangible and our world became barbed-wired, barricaded and curfewed. Armed soldiers of the Argyll and Sutherland Highlanders patrolled, while bulletproof vehicles transported forces people to work and school.

Just before the outbreak of warfare, my father was transferred to a position in Cyprus and our family exchanged one beautiful but troubled country for another.

My heart sank the day my mother showed me a newspaper article reporting on the 1967 Aden Insurgency. There was a photograph of a group of terrorists holding up a banner for the Front for the Liberation of South Yemen. In the centre of the photo, holding a Kalashnikov rifle, and with his fingerless hand in a triumphant salute ... was Jesus.

My mother had always been a good judge of character.

Always be a little kinder than necessary.

J.M. BARRIE

UNWOUND

Garrick Batten

It seemed like everything was going wrong. So, even if I was not royalty, to finally check into this Buenos Aires hotel and collapse on one of the two king-sized beds felt like success.

It started in Auckland with a hold-up in another long security queue because a voluble African would not listen. Well, it actually started earlier at roadworks and a lollipop man not coordinated with his mate around the corner. Then a queue at the Aerolineas Argentinas check-in counter. A maze of multicoloured suitcases, parcels, packs and pushchairs. The welcoming counter girl waited patiently while I found my passport. I'd forgotten I'd put it carefully in a jacket pocket separate from other travel documents. Everything seemed to conspire against me so I'd miss my plane. Of course I didn't, as airlines insist on three hours' check-in. I spent an hour sitting in the departure lounge tapping fingers, rechecking my ticket, listening for my boarding call above the crowded chatter of mutual trust in the miracle of flight. But all of us locked in individual cocoons of varied apprehension at the prospect of hurtling at 35,000 feet towards yesterday. Were laughs humorous or nervous? Eventually we pounded along the boarding ramp like lambs at the freezing works.

After I struggled down the aisle of people, parcels and bags I found a smiling young woman in my ticketed seat. I knew my ticket was correct, but then so was hers. The harried purser responded to my jabbed call button, flipped a coin and she was spirited away to business class. It should have been me, dressed in my best R.M. Williams business clothes for this trip. But instead I spent thirteen hours with an oversized, boring, snoring fellow who never even gave me his name. So it wasn't a surprise to wait for my now battered suitcase last onto the carousel. Once through immigration and customs, only one taxi remained under the floodlights, driven by a pirate descendant. I was physically and emotionally whacked. Not in a good state for my Argentine trip to get markets for our superior cattle genetics.

Argentinians eat late — very late — and the hotel restaurant off the lobby vibrated with a noisy, cheerful bustle of waiters, diners, food and drink. But after overfeeding to maximize airline offerings, bed seemed the best option to restore my body clock. I tossed and turned, thrashing in the sheets, but frustration and exhaustion flew me to universal dreamland. Driving a shiny black police car in reckless pursuit of something, but I didn't know what. Rain. Road skiddingly wet, people everywhere, a whooping siren and banging noises. Banging on my door. Siren. A fire siren. *Whoop! Whoop!* Hotel fire. Television memory images of hotel fires flashed as I struggled into a hotel bathrobe because I never wore pyjamas. Feet thrust into untied shoes, I joined a clamouring guest column in various states of dress and undress, sleep and awake, hurrying scurrying to the stairs. A horrible, burnt chemical smell. It seemed a long way down from the third floor and at the bottom a noisy throng was jamming the door to the street. We were driven out by flaming danger from the office behind the reception desk, but fighting incoming firemen with their equipment and hoses. All a shambles shouted in unintelligible Spanish.

The crowd swarmed in the road, shivered, exchanged rueful glances with fellow guests, teeth and words chattering. We were let back in after an hour or so, many now goose-pimpled and purple with cold. Still tasting smoke. The fire had been confined to the office in a mess of water, broken and burnt furniture, and computers.

No lifts. I climbed back to the third floor on stairs besieged by a caterpillar of shoving, upset guests. Pungent smoke lingered. In the long corridor, dimly lit by emergency lighting, all doors looked the same apart from the number. I couldn't remember my room number and now the door was locked. My room card sat in the light switch slot in my room — whichever it was. No good going back to the office shambles to ask. I seemed to remember mine being somewhere in the middle, but which one? The chilled excitement of fire evacuation on top of exhaustion just added to my confusion.

If not my room, perhaps I could use the connecting door from the next room that was a feature of this hotel. In desperation I knocked, and the door was ripped open by a towering man who abused me in Spanish, then slammed it shut. Obviously not my room.

I tried another door. Locked. No response. Perhaps mine? I knocked on the next door. Another man wrapped in a floral dressing gown, smiling until he saw who it was.

I gave up, turning to stumble back downstairs for help when a door on the other side of the corridor swung open and a nightgown-clad young woman grabbed my arm. I could feel her body warmth through my bathrobe I was so cold. And she was so close. Startled would be a complete understatement.

'*Senor, senor! Por favor, por favor!*'

I could only respond, 'What's wrong?'

'Oh — English!'

'Well … New Zealand actually.'

'Please please 'elp me. Dark. No light. Alone. *Asustado.*'

I didn't know what *asustado* meant but I got the message from her clutching fingers and imploring eyes, which I could dimly see in the gloom.

'Please, please *senor.*' She tried to pull me into her room.

'Well we could open the curtains to let in some street light. Would that help?'

At the window I groped for cords to the heavy brocade drapes, and then harsh street neon. I guessed my distressed damsel was a slim woman in her thirties, her eyes framed by long black hair as she wrapped herself protectively in a blanket.

Now my turn to ask for help. I tried to explain my predicament about losing my room with nowhere to sleep. And being cold. I had to be careful not to abuse sympathy but had no other option.

I'm not sure how much she understood but she became the perfect hostess.

She thrust a blanket at me. 'You sleep here. That bed. Two big beds — *ridiculo!*' She paused with what seemed like embarrassment at what she was suggesting. 'A little drink for cold — *si?*'

And then she fled to the bathroom but returned wafting perfume, hair brushed, now in a ponytail.

I had been pacing around, frustrated at loss of independence, uneasy in her company until she patted the bed beside her. The constant changes in the street neon blue-green-red-orange colour created an almost disco date.

I opened the minibar and we explored, sampled the contents and gradually cleared the shelves. We were trying to exchange life stories as we talked down the excitement and worries of the last few hours. She struggled to pronounce Alistair so I became Al. She introduced herself as Alvira, and I correctly guessed a dancer from long legs occasionally flashing through a blanket slip and the way she stood with positioned feet. She was on a one-night stopover on the way south to perform at a prestigious polo club.

We probably understood only about half of what we told each other sitting on her bed. We had some common words, but hands and smiles talk a lot. Our ringless fingers established no current relationships, and fingers counted ages. As the room cooled with no heating, we huddled closer on her bed and sent body messages.

It wasn't easy to get across to an obviously city girl when I tried to explain about how we bred cattle on our farm, but I think she understood about a cattle ranch. We'd concentrated on specifically selecting for important easy calving, and it was those genetics I was hoping to sell.

She wouldn't have appreciated how difficult it was going to be to sell cattle genetics from little New Zealand to Argentina, one of the biggest cattle countries. But we had longstanding connections. I had shared a Lincoln University class with a guy from Mendoza years ago. And the All Blacks still played the Pumas.

When I started to talk about selling semen without knowing the appropriate Spanish words, I tried talking with my hands but it all got too embarrassing. The technical terms were beyond us. I think she probably understood much later when wrapping those long legs, and bare skin on bare skin as the best way to keep warm.

As a climax to a long night it was impossible to order breakfast for two with no office, no phone and no room service. But we had survived the night — together.

They say that travel broadens the mind and wisdom comes with age. I grew up quickly that night, and was even relaxed for the first time on that trip. Helped by Argentine hospitality and female kindness.

A little **thought** and a little kindness are often worth more than a great deal of money.

JOHN RUSKIN

THE CARER

Hugh Major

Out of nowhere, a bang-on impact, a jet of pain in the leg. I'm thrown to the road where recoiling from the smash is an involuntary twisting, causing a clumping of the busted limb from side to side — broken bones hauled over by a still-intact envelope of skin. Who's that yelling into the night air? It's me. Desperate, rational faculties check on movement of the toes, of motor functions. Horizontal, I can only see the night sky. Voices of people, gathering, zoom in and out.

... the motorcycle I'd borrowed, headlights of a sudden swerving car ...

A face comes down, businesslike, practical. It's a doctor. 'You're just going to get some pain relief.' There's a jab in the arm and a skyrocketing up, out of the broken body to a little stratosphere of bliss, the leg no more than a memory, turned to ribbon and undulating off, south over Otahuhu. Far below, the circular sweep of an ambulance's red light ... but it's just a brief escape. The smallest impulse or intent allows a smooth drop back into the body, painless for a time before the pethidine loses its authority. Then the sting comes pulsing back, and the condition — disabled, entrapped.

Somewhere in the hospital basement a surgeon leans over, assuring imminent release (from restless writhing). He jokes that no surgical saw is being prepared. The evening's second needle goes in, coolness spreads up the arm, then blankness.

Awake, in an orthopaedic ward. There are three other victims of road accidents, also a Polynesian boy and a World War I veteran with a helium balloon in shiny crimson attached to his wheelchair, as though its ribbon will soon be cut, his soul borne aloft. I look down at my leg, encased in thick new plaster from groin to instep. It turns out the femur, fractured in two places, now has an intermedullary 'K-rod' (profound thanks to the ingenuity of Küntscher's supportive nail) hammered down inside the marrow. Below the knee, tibia and fibula are both crushed, their splinters held by the grip of plaster to begin knitting. Flat on my back, the leg as heavy as cement, I wait and weaken.

After the pethidine, pre-med and general anaesthetic, comes the drug trolley — daily nostrums with their gift of headaches and insomnia.

I wake, disoriented, into darkness. There's a bass note of portentous music, regular as a heartbeat. It stops. There's a scream, followed by a moan of fear from far off. Where on earth is this? The Underworld? It's the Sunday Horrors, the beds of keen viewers having been trundled to a telly in the next ward. The onscreen scream triggered some trauma in a patient down the corridor … exclamations from television's gothic drama finding echoes in the hospital's restless sleepers.

In the bed on one side of me is a man who said he'd stopped at a motorway offramp to retrieve what he thought were company papers lying in the road. That was the last thing he remembered before cartwheeling over the bonnet of an approaching car and punching a hole through the windscreen.

On the other side is a man who spends most of the day asleep, hospital blanket pulled up to his chin and his mouth open as if ready to receive the sacrament. His wife visits daily, approaching his bed in trepidation as though its open-mouthed occupant has already slipped away.

Only half-hidden behind a drawn curtain a nurse flings off bedclothes and gown in a businesslike way to assist the Polynesian boy. He's embarrassed at being exposed. She responds, 'Don't worry love, I've seen enough of those to make a picket fence between here and Wellington.'

Patients, drugged and debilitated, need to find their own reserves of strength, patience and humour — something the grapes, cards and small talk of visitors can rarely achieve. But what about when this help comes from the outside, unexpectedly — from someone who can offer more than the weight of a doctor's or nurse's professional assessment?

In the ward's long tunnel of waiting, of getting used to immobility, of ordering ceiling tiles into patterns and listening to the same tapes on the Walkman, I feel a hand on my arm. It's a woman, olive skinned, middle aged, her long hair pulled back and held under a silk scarf. She takes my hand in both of hers, looks at me, like a mother, directly but not intrusively, reads my worn-down state and says: 'Don't worry — a higher power is looking after you.' It could have been some platitude on a Hallmark sympathy card, but the calm assurance in her words floods her face, and her eyes convey the same message. It seems she makes an appeal to part of myself that already knows what she says but would otherwise have no access to it — as though years of secular conditioning have cast doubt on a higher state of love and connectedness. That single verbal encouragement was enough; the real reassurance is in her presence. She tells me her name: Mrs Fernandez. Did I ask her for it? I can't remember. Her leaving is something of which I'm barely conscious, but the munificence, the generosity, remains. Who was she? An ordinary hospital visitor? Why did she choose me? Was she approaching other patients and offering encouragement? The simple morale-boosting of 'you're being looked after' could have been the words of a priest, or in her case a nun, but as the speaker or conduit she was just as much the higher power — both messenger and the very helper she referred to.

Mrs Fernandez's few words linger for days afterwards. She supplied a missing but necessary component of care and recuperation — recognition that there is a mental and spiritual dimension to a person as well as a physical or mechanical one. Re-aligning and clamping fractured bone is just the basic, outer aspect of recovery.

A fortnight goes by. Room service at the health department's hotel is punctual but the culinary standard low. My arms are looking thinner and I'm impatient with the slowness of osteo-amalgamation. Here comes the final operation where a new cast will be fitted with a hinge to begin movement of the knee. It's back downstairs to white walls, chrome trolleys, surgeons' pale green scrubs and needles. I'm on a trolley in some subterranean corridor; there's not long till the intravenous seethe of anaesthetic … and beyond that, lumping heavy plaster around on crutches …

There's a hand on my arm.

She arrived from nowhere. How did she know I was here and at this final stage of treatment? How did she get to this restricted zone, adjacent to the operating theatres?

'You're always in the hands of God — that is your strength.'

Is it lifted straight from Christian scripture? No matter; she makes it sound real and relevant, while my conditioned, sensible self is saying: *This is nice but just wishful thinking. You've had a traffic accident and life sucks. Furthermore, ultimately you're going to die, so come on, get used to it.*

Mrs Fernandez's look of sweet accord seems permanent. This is her nature. As before, her ministering words seem to remain in the air, as if reflected back by the walls' white sheen. She leans in. Time slows. I am fully focused on her. In normal life, in the outer world, there's precious little time or cause for this connection, this intimacy.

After the engagement she seems to drift off, in no direction, my hand released, and because I'm gazing straight up at the ceiling tiles, she could have vanished into a lateral abyss. But her little whirlpool of words remains, recurring, reinforcing itself.

❧

At first there's just a bright, horizontal line, but as it comes into focus I can see something being held in front of me. What seems to be a chromium pipe, and someone's leaning down, displaying it between two fingers. It's a kind of trophy — what's been walking around in my femur for eighteen months and can now see the light of day. On a closer view it's about 18 inches long, like a sickle moon when viewed end-on, a hole drilled through to draw it out of the bone and compressed at the same end where the hammer drove it in. It's salutary to think of how many legs it would have saved in the two world wars.

People marvel at the orthopaedic trophy. It's amazing, they say, what technology and medicine can achieve, the nurses, the doctors, surgeons ...

Yes, and there was someone else ...

Wherever there is a
human being, there is
an opportunity
for a kindness.

LUCIUS ANNAEUS SENECA

WHEN THE TERRORISTS ATTACKED OUR HOME

Sultan Somjee

I was seven years old when the terrorists attacked our home. We lived in an isolated house in Eastleigh on the outskirts of Nairobi. It was a stone house surrounded by a 12-foot-high bamboo fence that my grandfather had built to keep away hyenas from the forested Mathare River valley about 10 kilometres away. Behind the house was the 30-feet-high thorn fence of the St Teresa's Catholic mission and then, then, there were no other buildings or trees around.

Around mid 1951, we began hearing about an insurgency brewing in Kenya. The elders talked about it on their evening walks. In the same breath, they talked about India's recently ended 100-year-long freedom movement and the violence it entailed. Sometimes, I accompanied my grandfather on his walks with his peers because his vision was failing and he had difficulties seeing in the evening. A year later, in 1952, the governor declared the state of emergency. It was then we learnt that the gang that had attacked our house was called the Mau Mau, a freedom movement against British colonialism in Kenya. I feared as much as I hated the Mau

Mau. To me they were the terrorists who had looted our home and terrified us.

It was around 2 a.m. in the dead of night when I heard the door break like there was an explosion. The crash that seemed to come out of pitch darkness shocked me out of my sleep. It was so intense that even today, more than half a century later, I cringe every time I hear a door slammed. A rock jumped twice on the floor and landed near my bed. Splinters of wood weighed down on my mosquito net like a haul of shells and shrimps in a fisherman's net. We lived in one room. We were a family of five: my parents, my elder brother, my four-year-old sister and me. The revolutionaries entered immediately. It all happened at once: the bang, the rock, wood splinters flying about the room, and then the phantom faces, their bewildered eyes and sweaty faces set in black wiry dreadlocks. I felt their looks pressing me down. Like ants, they spread around the room with clubs and machetes. One stood over my mother with a club and another over my father with a machete. A smell like that of caged jungle animals at the zoo filled the room. Later, it was reported on the radio that a contingent of the Mau Maus lived in the caves of the Mathare Valley and that the residents of Eastleigh were asked to immediately report any suspicious character to the police. The guerrillas who roamed from late evenings to dawn were in two groups: forest guerrillas who mostly attacked white plantation owners, and urban guerrillas who attacked residences in the towns. We were, most probably, attacked by the urban guerrillas.

At that moment of horror of the attack on our house, all I saw were the terrorists' bloody eyes scuttling about the room, impatient and jumpy like a flock of trapped birds. When one of them looked at me, I felt stabbed. I saw my father dragged across the room and tied to a chair. They gagged my parents with dirty socks left for washing in a bucket. My brother and I sat back to back on one bed, terrified. Our backs were wet, absorbing each other's sweat. I continued looking down, pressing my chin to my chest and calling on God to help, while all the time I felt bloodshot eyes tearing into me.

They started emptying clothes and whatever there was from the cupboards. From under the heap of clothes they had made on the floor, my sister's doll cried musically, which fascinated one of them. He stood there momentarily and then picked up the pink plastic English doll and began turning it over, listening to the melodic note from its perforated back. Hearing the sound of her doll crying, my little sister woke up suddenly, bright eyed in wonder, smiling and talking excitedly as four year olds do, chattering to herself, and walking round her cot holding the bars of the metal frame. Then she stopped and watched, her eyes widened, inquisitively, puzzled at what was happening.

'My *dhingly* doll!' she wailed in Swahili. 'I want my *dhingly* doll.' She began crying and looking around for Mother.

The General, as I heard them calling their leader, turned around and looked at my sister. His bloodshot eyes stilled on her. I froze. He was over 6 feet tall. He stood there like a giant by the cot. He had his palms on his hips, arms akimbo. Then his red eyes softened like a father's eyes put to the child appealing for a favour.

'Don't take the little girl's *ka-rendi*, and anything else that belongs to this child,' he instructed his men.

When finally the Mau Mau left after what seemed like a night of plunder and terror, they had taken everything in the house that they could carry. My clothes, shoes and even my Lego set was gone. But there was a pile of dresses, toys and shoes left behind on the floor. The revolutionaries had left behind everything that belonged to my little sister.

❄

Years went by. The horrific propaganda against the Mau Mau lessened, and the story of the attack on our home faded into a distant nightmare. Kenya became independent in 1963. We celebrated liberation from colonial rule and the end of racism only to pave a way for nationalism and brutal dictatorships that followed. I completed my high school, joined the university, went overseas to do postgraduate studies and returned in the early 1970s to join the University of Nairobi as a research fellow in material culture. I was interested in Africa's indigenous cultures and its history from 'the people's point of view'. I had started leaning towards socialism and joined the rural theatre that was an outfit of the underground against the despot Jomo Kenyatta.

I worked with the communities of peasants, farm and factory workers in an area that was known as the hub of the Mau Mau. I came across former Mau Mau fighters and almost everyone had a relative in the anti-colonial organization. Ironically, the first play, *Ngaahika Ndeenda* (I Will Marry When I Want), that we put up was about the Mau Mau. The experience had an impact on me, for I began to think differently about the Mau Mau. They were no longer the wild terrorists who had looted and traumatized me and my family but revolutionaries fighting for liberation from colonialism. In fact, they became heroes in my young man's mind. I read everything I could lay my hands on about the Mau Mau. I even drew them from photographs. The frightful images of their eyes in my mind changed to those of heroic warriors with idealism shining on their faces that spoke of sacrifice for freedom and human dignity.

Today, as I turn 75, my mind sometimes immerses in reflections from the past that come and go like waves of an ocean washing so vast a shore of my lifetime. There are thoughts on the good deeds and bad deeds I have done. Some fill me with pride about my achievements, and some with sadness about my deceits and failures. Some are full of fear and even hate that sometimes I speak out loudly to myself in abuses hurled at someone or something. Self-talk, I have come to accept, comes with ageing in some people. Sometimes, a dream from my childhood returns in a scream. The sound of the door crashing down on me has stayed with me. The image of the bloodshot eyes of the Mau Mau revisits me. Sigmund Freud would call them childhood memories in my subconscious and construct a theory around it to write an essay on my personality. However, when awake and with a conscious mind, when I talk about the night the Mau Mau attacked our house in Eastleigh in Nairobi, when I was seven years old, I speak about the compassion of the leader they called the General. How he looked at my four-year-old sister and kindness filled his bloodshot eyes even as he held the deadly machete in one hand.

I speak about this incident as a reflection on humanity that I have come to know we all have in us. That even the fiercest looking people from other countries, other cultures and other religions that we see or hear about in the media as enemies carry compassion in their hearts.

One day, I wish to write a story for children called 'When the terrorists attacked our home'.

Faith is taking the first step, even when you don't see the whole staircase.

MARTIN LUTHER KING, JR

FAITH ACCOMPLI

Terry Callan

We were off on a beautiful early summer morning on our little adventure. We were to drive inland to Clones in county Monaghan, a journey of an hour and a half from our home town Dundalk in county Louth. It being the first public holiday of summer, we'd decided to take a little trip and have a nice day out but we had a reason for choosing this particular destination.

We were going there to see a faith healer in the hope that he might be able help my wife, who had been suffering from chronic sinusitis for more than a year. A debilitating condition that would often see her having to spend hours in a darkened room in order to get some relief from the blinding headaches from which she suffered. Sometimes the doctor would have to visit our home and give my wife an injection to relieve the swelling in her face and eyes. Other days it would just sit there like a flickering flame ready to flare up at a moment's notice. She'd taken all the recommended medicine and treatments without relief. At our latest consultation the doctor told us the next step would be to have an operation that may or may not be successful in eliminating the condition and that my wife could be on medication indefinitely.

So it was against this background that we set off on our little trip in the hope that Donal the faith healer would be able to help us. Faith healers in Ireland were part of the fabric of society and were revered by some and ridiculed by others as nothing more than charlatans. My opinion stood somewhere in the middle of this group. Said to be the seventh son of a seventh son and to have the 'gift' of healing by the laying of hands or the administration of herbal medicines. They were said to have 'the cure' for anything from warts to shingles and even, in some cases, cancer. Even though the trip was my idea I was and always remained sceptical of such powers being bestowed on anyone, but in the circumstances we found ourselves in I was keeping an open mind and would be happy to be proved wrong. My wife, on the other hand, was open and even enthusiastic about the concept, which of course may well have been of great advantage to the whole process.

The Irish countryside was in full bloom as we trundled along in our trusty old Ford Anglia. The meadows awash with wildflowers, resplendent in the sun-dappled green fields. The hedgerows lit up with honeysuckle and elder and a myriad of shrubs made for a very pleasant journey indeed. There was no appointment to be made, no secretary to take down details, just simply turn up and present yourself. Neither was there any charge, though a charitable donation would be appreciated.

We arrived at our destination, the little town of Clones, in late morning. The plan, if you could call it such, was to ask some of the locals where the faith healer lived, as we didn't know the exact address. If we had any misconceptions about being able to find someone who would be able to point us in the right direction they were soon dissipated by the first person we asked. He was happy to give us detailed instructions on how to get there, informing us that 'sure whatever it is that ails ye sure he'll get rid of it in no time at all'. I got the feeling that the locals were very proud of their famous faith healer.

So off we went with our directions and sure enough we soon found the house of the faith healer. It was a little whitewashed cottage atop a hill along a narrow country road. We were surprised at first by the absence of people, as we expected to have to wait our turn, perhaps in a queue. I approached the house, which stood behind an iron gate, the kind used to move livestock or machinery through. As I did, my senses were accosted by a veritable soup of fragrances of wildflowers, shrubbery, animal smells. The sound of insects busily pollinating the flowers and shrubs. An old goat considered me inquisitively for a moment before going about his business. Everything was so peaceful and quiet, the air so fresh I wondered for a moment if perhaps this was Donal's secret. Get people out in the fresh country air and all their ailments would vanish in an instant. As I approached the gate I noticed a sign which read: 'We apologize that Donal is unavailable today as he is unwell and has been taken to hospital.'

How ironic, I thought, *that the man we sought to put our faith in had gone to put his faith in medical science*. Oh well, I suppose even faith healers are prone to illness now and again. I went back to the car and told my wife the news and her thoughts were less of disappointment for her own predicament but more of compassion for the unfortunate faith healer, which was typical of her nature.

At least the day was still young and we still had our picnic. We found a nice park near Monaghan town with a pond and some ducks. The sun warmed us as we laid our blanket out for our picnic. There were sandwiches and cake and drinks and the kids finished off feeding the ducks and chasing butterflies, a task which brought them a great deal of joy. Mum and Dad sat watching their kids with no less joy. The fun at an end, it was time to pack up and go. On the way home, I suggested to my wife that we call in to visit a cathedral on the outskirts of Monaghan town.

St Macartan's Cathedral dominates the skyline around Monaghan town. I had passed it many times as my work demanded, and had often admired its sheer scale and magnificence. We passed through the manicured gardens and the statues of the saints on the outside walls and through the large oak doorways. The inside of the cathedral was no less impressive with its gothic arches and stained glass windows and a magnificently carved white granite altar that stretched fully one third of the length of the cathedral. I tried to imagine it in all its pomposity, with bishops and clergy, a choir and congregation. It must be a sight to behold. At that moment, though, we had it all to ourselves except for a few parishioners and some ladies fixing flowers on the altar.

We sat in silent prayer for some moments while we admired the surroundings.

Then it was time to go home. The kids quickly fell asleep in the back of the car as we drove along. I asked my wife what she thought of the cathedral and she said she loved it and was delighted we got to see it. She also told me that while we were there she offered up a prayer for the faith healer so that he may get well. A lovely gesture, I thought; wouldn't it be wonderful if her prayers were able to help the very person to whom we had reached out to help us?

The bright summer sunshine was giving way to twilight when we arrived home and after a quick meal we got the kids off to bed where they quickly fell asleep, tired from their exertions. We'd had a wonderful day out with our little family and even though our primary objective hadn't been achieved — to see the faith healer — we were well pleased with our day out in the Irish countryside. It occurred to me that the heavily pollinated air may have irritated my wife's condition so I asked how she felt and she remarked that she felt better than she had for a long time.

It has been more than 30 years since that day out with our little family. I think of it often; you see, my wife has never since suffered any symptoms of sinusitis. No blinding headaches. No swollen eyes. No blocked nasal passages or visits to the doctor. If on the day in question my wife had seen the faith healer and he had laid his hands on her or given her some herbal concoction or ointment, then I would be heralding the power of suggestion working its wonders on her fragile mind. But there was no laying of hands or herbal remedy, just a silent prayer offered up in selfless compassion for a stranger she had never met.

While my opinion of the faith healing process is still that of sceptical acceptance with an open mind, I am however compelled by the events of that day and the subsequent 'miracle' of my wife's healing to have an unshakable belief in the power of prayer.

Walk with the dreamers, the believers, the courageous, the cheerful, the planners, the doers, the successful people with their heads in the clouds and their feet on the ground. Let their spirit ignite a fire within you to leave this world better than when you found it ...

WILFRED PETERSON

AMRITA

Barbara Krefel

As we entered the local community hall the excited Tibetan chatter became subdued. There were twelve of us who had volunteered as mentors to the newly arrived Tibetan refugees. We were an eclectic mob who had bonded over the month of intensive training. Recently retired, I had spotted the article in the *Manly Daily* which appealed for an urgent need of mentors for the refugees. As my daughter had on several occasions worked in a Nepalese orphanage where she came into contact with many Tibetans, I felt a connection.

After a delicious lunch of momos (dumplings) and damje (sweet rice), prepared by the Tibetans, each mentor was paired up with the most suitable mentee. Amongst the mentees there was a sick, ageing monk, a young married couple, a middle-aged woman who made the best momos, two young men in their twenties and a tall monk with a beautiful smile, who although still only in his thirties was regarded as highly spiritually advanced.

As our names were called out a feeling of anxiety came over me. I was aware that most of the mentees had experienced highly traumatic events and I questioned how I would cope with the impact these events would have had on their physical and emotional health. At last my name was called out and mentee

Amrita, a slight girl, eighteen years old, shyly stepped forward. She held, high at shoulder height, a beautiful white silk *khata* (scarf), bowed and presented it to me as a sign of greeting and respect.

Amrita had been adopted by her maternal aunt and her husband when she was ten years old and went to live with them in Dharamsala, India. Amrita now considered them her parents. Her adopted father had suffered many years of torture in Chinese jails on religious grounds and after his release had worked for the Dalai Lama in Dharamsala. When he and his wife were accepted as humanitarian refugees to Australia in 2014, Amrita was not allowed to travel with them due to a technical bungle over her adoption status. Her father, now 70 years old and in fragile health, fought for two years to get permission for Amrita to join them.

At least once a week I met up with Amrita at the unit she shared with her parents. The small lounge was set up as a Buddhist shrine. Above a bronze statue of Buddha was a photo of the charismatic, smiling Dalai Lama. To the left was a bell symbolizing the Buddha's enlightened mind and, to the right, a text symbolizing his enlightened speech. Offerings of flowers, incense and food were placed on the shrine and in the tradition called *yonchap*, seven small brass bowls were filled at sunrise with water and emptied at sunset. This is to cultivate generosity and to serve as an antidote to attachment and greed.

I helped Amrita with basic things such as banking, how to get public transport to college and with her English studies. She was nervous and hesitant at the beginning, and told me that she suffered from stomach problems. However, her concept of English impressed me and I saw an intelligence and inner strength beyond her years. I learnt to be a good listener and soon realized that time had a different meaning in both cultures.

The Tibetans are a proud and polite race and after spending three hours with them it was not until I got up to leave that Amrita would tell me the issue that was troubling them. Both parents had little command of English so she immediately became their interpreter, accompanying them to medical and dental appointments.

At first I thought our meetings were a little tense when her father was present, as he was fiercely protective of her and it took time for him to trust that my support was genuine.

Amrita and I then started meeting up at the beach and during our long walks a close bond was formed. As we walked, breathing in the salty mist, I heard her dreams and desires for the future but also her fears — that she wasn't clever enough — or her concerns that her father might not approve. It was a balancing act. On one hand I encouraged her and built up her self-esteem, telling her that she was intelligent and could achieve her ambitions, on the other hand I had to respect her father and be non-judgmental.

On one particular occasion Amrita's father asked what I would suggest as suitable career paths for her. With each suggestion he became more agitated. Childcare: 'She would be blamed if anything happened to the children'. Nursing: 'Physically too hard for her'. Every suggestion was met with fear.

Through Amrita as translator we discussed the differences of careers in Australia compared to in India. I assured him I was only a sounding board and in the end they would both have to be happy with her career choice.

I felt dejected as I left for home.

The following week I was surprised that there had been a big shift in trust. Photos were brought out of happy shots of the family with the Dalai Lama and of Amrita's mother hand weaving exquisite silk carpets in India. They persuaded me to drink their traditional tea. It was extremely salty and sweet at the same time and as I took a mouthful, with three pairs of eyes intently waiting for my reaction, I couldn't help but screw up my face. We all burst out laughing. The Tibetans have a wonderful sense of humour and I found that laughing together was not only a real tension release but an excellent bonding tool.

A year had passed when Amrita asked me to join her at the library to show me her major assignment before she presented it at college. It was to be a bullet point presentation of her life to date. As I read the lines, I struggled to contain my emotions, trying to comprehend the fear she must have experienced as a ten year old and admiring the courage it took to keep going.

TIBET
- Born 1997 in Samdup
- One of seven children
- My family were nomads and farmers
- We had sheep, goats, yaks and crops
- Life was peaceful. People were satisfied with what their land provided
- Learnt to read and write
- Mum and Dad adopted me at age ten

- I moved to Lhasa to live with Aunty and Uncle

LHASA TO NEPAL
- We escaped to Nepal
- One guide + one nun + six girls
- To Nepal border by Jeep
- Walked two days at night
  - No torch
  - Holding hands
  - Sharp stones (sore feet)
  - Cold wind
  - Hid during the day
  - Crept across the border to Nepal at night

NEPAL TO INDIA
- Delayed for three months at Nepal reception centre
- Bus to India via Bhutan
- Arrived in Dharamsala to live with my adopted parents

I paused and thought about my daughters at ten years of age. How carefree and uncomplicated their lives were, secure in a land of sunshine.

As I read on about her studies in Dharamsala, culminating in the Year 12 Leaving Certificate I felt the determination and inner strength Amrita possessed.

'That's wonderful Amrita! You have expressed so well your life in a few words.' Her head was now held high and the gaze from her almond brown eyes direct.

Over time an ease opened up between us. After driving her home from a beach picnic we had with my granddaughters, I asked her, 'How did you feel when you left your mother at just ten years old?'

'I was excited about the adventure. My mother had seven children and her sister had none. It is common to give a child to a relative in Tibet. We don't have the same attachment as I have seen here between children and their mothers.'

I nodded, thinking how wise and intuitive this young girl was.

The need for our meetings became less as the months passed, until it dwindled to the odd text message. I have to admit I felt deflated, similar to when my daughters left home.

However, upon reflection I realized independence and self-sufficiency are the keys to success. Amrita is now a confident young Australian with many new friends and a part-time job, and is studying advanced English.

The biggest gift was mine. I have had the privilege of being given a small window into how another culture perceives the world. To live in harmony we must be non-judgmental, respecting the cultural and religious/spiritual beliefs of others. Shared humour, trust and love enriches our lives.

This morning I was walking along the local shopping centre when I heard someone call out my name.

It was Amrita, with her beautiful beaming smile. We hugged and I asked about her studies.

'I am starting my nursing degree next week,' she answered with great pride.

Gentleness
and kindness
will make
our homes
a paradise
upon earth.

C.A. BARTOL

THE LAST GIFT

Yvonne Blackwood

Scotty was a wee man, probably 4 feet 10 inches, but he was a powerhouse of energy. Having emigrated from Scotland when he was a mere boy, Scotty's accent remained as thick as pea soup. I met him one summer's evening when he came to help a friend collect the bedroom furniture I was giving away. Smiling with a twinkle in his blue eyes, he inquired why I was giving away the furniture, declaring that it was in excellent condition. The question suggested that Scotty did not understand that women become tired of things now and again, that they need to have new things. This I explained. Another smile, then he asked if I needed a handyman. Well of course I did; all single women need one, especially if they are more than 60 years old. He gave me his card. 'Call me anytime you need help with anything,' he said.

The front yard of the house was postage stamp sized. The grass craggy, patchy and difficult to mow. It did not matter what was done to make it lush, it remained an eyesore. I contacted Scotty to see what else could be done with it. After discussing different options, I decided to have the grass removed and to cover the area with river stones. Scotty felt that some greenery and colour would make it more attractive and placed four flat, decorative slabs at intervals among the river stones. He suggested that I place potted flowers on the slabs. He also made a garden bed around the small oak tree in the centre of the yard.

The next summer several neighbours stopped by to admire my beautiful front yard. Colourful annuals covered the flowerbed around the oak tree and the painted flowerpots placed on the slabs embedded among the river stones sprawled with annuals too. Every year I incorporated a different colour scheme — yellow and purple, pink and white, red and white. I enjoyed my little grassless garden.

Scotty had made his mark; he was thoughtful, helpful and full of ideas. He became my go-to guy for every small chore around the house. Among other things, he trimmed the few bushes in the backyard, painted the garage door, installed a storm door at the back door and changed the track light bulbs in the kitchen several times.

The wonderful thing about Scotty is he never rushed when he visited. We would sit at the dining table and talk for hours about everything topical, except anything to do with religion — he didn't want to hear or talk about that. Many times Scotty came bearing gifts — Lindor (my favourite chocolate), a special hook to hang my handbag, a box of dozens of garbage bags. One Christmas, he spent time hunting through stores for a hand-crafted mistletoe which he presented to me, pleased as the cat that ate the canary.

The day Scotty installed the storm door at the back of the house he asked for a piece of foil. I climbed up on one of the dining room chairs to reach the top kitchen cupboard shelf where I kept the foil. The next time Scotty visited he arrived with a large cardboard box. He presented the box to me saying, 'I don't want to see you climbing up on any chair. The next thing, you'll fall and break your neck!' Inside the box was a sturdy, lightweight two-tier step ladder. Scotty's acts of kindness never failed to amaze me and I always wondered why he did them.

But the ultimate act of kindness was yet to come. During one of our tête-à-têtes, I had mentioned to Scotty that I would like to build a deck in the backyard one day, to which he replied, 'I can build it for you. I have a lot of experience building decks. One of my sons is an expert at building decks.' I told him I did not have the funds to build it that year.

Next spring, as soon as the April and early May showers had dissipated, Scotty arrived one Saturday morning. 'Let's go to Lowes and get an estimate for your deck,' he said. I had not given any further thought to the deck since we spoke about it the previous year, but what was I to do when the deck-builder exhibited such enthusiasm? He drove me to Lowes, we received estimates for different options, and with a little pressure from Scotty I ordered the materials — you see, he had an account at Lowes and he offered to use his Lowes card for the purchase and by so doing, I received a discount. I saved almost $300. I repaid Scotty's invoice by the time his bill arrived.

Scotty had confided in me a year earlier that he had been diagnosed with colon cancer, had received chemotherapy and the cancer had gone into remission. While he was building the deck I observed that he moved slower than normal and he took breaks often. He worked alone, except for one day when a female worker assisted him. He did not complain, therefore I assumed his lack of energy was due to the heat; besides, deck-building is strenuous work. Within five days, Scotty completed a beautiful, professional deck, one I am very proud of.

Scotty built for me a delightful wooden planter with the leftover wood from the deck and coated it with earth-brown stain to match the composite boards. It fitted perfectly at the side of the deck. Together, we filled it with rich soil and repotted the clematis he had to remove from the side of the fence in order to build the deck. The planter was his last gift to me. He passed away four days after completing his work — he knew he was dying but was determined to build the deck for me before he died.

Much to my astonishment, I learnt from reading his obituary that the wee man who I thought was in his early seventies was 86 years old! Every time I relax in the loveseat on the deck, shaded by the patio umbrella, Scotty's wee frame always comes to mind. I miss him.

LOVE & LOSS

ISBN 978-1-925820-07-2

SUCCESS

STRUGGLE &

TIMELESS WISDOM
True stories that reveal the depths of the human experience

STRUGGLE & SUCCESS

ISBN 978-1-925820-08-9

FEAR & COURAGE

ISBN 978-1-925820-06-5